Twayne's English Authors Series

Sylvia E. Bowman, *Editor*

INDIANA UNIVERSITY

Gabriel Fielding

(TEAS) 162

GABRIEL FIELDING

GABRIEL FIELDING

By ALFRED BORRELLO

Kingsborough Community College of the
City University of New York

Twayne Publishers, Inc.   ::   New York

Library of Congress Cataloging in Publication Data

Borrello, Alfred.
  Gabriel Fielding.

  (Twayne's English authors series, TEAS 162)
  Bibliography: p. 155.
  1. Barnsley, Alan Gabriel. I. Title.
PR6003.A74Z6   823'.9'14   73–16101
ISBN 0–8057–1194–5

To
J.M.J.
AND
JUDE AND THERESA
AS I PROMISED

Preface

This first critical-analytical study of the novels of Gabriel Fielding is, of necessity, an orderly examination of his works. In this order, however, lurks the danger that the essential appeal of the books may be lost to view simply because the attraction any art holds for the viewer escapes absolute analysis; for art is more than the techniques applied, more than the subject matter treated, more than its patterns and the philosophy it reflects, just as we are more than the chemicals of which we are composed. I feel compelled, therefore, to indicate in some basic way the spell Fielding's novels have cast over me.

No one can hope to convey to another exactly, nor remotely, as I have come to learn, the pleasure a work of art offers to oneself. I can, nevertheless, suggest that joy afforded me by Fielding's books in a limited manner by way of an analogy, provided that the reader understand that my analogy at best is inexact. I liken the enjoyment I derive to a fine dinner served with the most exquisite of wines and the finest of china, linen, silver, candlelight and all the accoutrements of an elegant dining room. There is the joy of the first sip of wine, the first bite of food. There is the joy, when hunger at last satisfied, one can turn one's complete attention to the delicious *mélange* of flavors, the delights of the eye, the pleasures of good conversation matched only by the quality of the food. At last, when the dinner is over, the source of pleasure is left; and the diner takes with him the memories he has gathered which will be cherished for the future. And more fundamentally, perhaps unknown to him, the food has by delicate biological processes become part of himself. This is the end product of Fielding's novels.

I leave them knowing that they have given me great pleasure, yes, most certainly; but I leave them with a sense that they have become part of me and have altered in some essential manner what I once was. This alteration occurs in that portion one commonly calls the heart but is, more specifically, the soul.

Like all good artists, however, Fielding does not readily reveal the sources of his effectiveness which is his art. To arrive at an understanding of that art, one must dismember the work, its product. I have attempted to do that with as much delicacy as possible in order to preserve the total effect for which he strives. In addition, I have tried to clarify the development of his art by treating his writing chronologically. The reader should note a consistency in that development in terms of its themes and the methods that he applies to achieve the goals he establishes. The final chapter is devoted to an examination of his theories of literature.

The reader should also note a certain lack in this discussion. Nowhere are Fielding's short stories examined, and this omission is deliberate. In one way or another, they reflect some aspect of his novels; therefore, to examine them would be redundant. Some of his essays are examined, however, because he reveals in them something of the workings of his art. His poetry is also discussed (Chapter 1) because it clarifies the origins of those attitudes and methods from which he develops his novels. All references made to his novels are to American editions since English editions are not available in this country.

I am deeply indebted to Mr. Fielding and his gracious wife Edwina Cook Barnsley, for without their help this work would never have seen the light of day. I am especially grateful for the factual material they supplied through correspondence and conversations with me and for the delicacy with which they avoided shaping my views and opinions. This book also could never have been produced had not Mr. John Willey of the William Morrow and Company, the American publishers of Mr. Fielding's books, given me free access to his files.

I am also indebted to Dr. Frank Towne who willingly permitted me to see his own study of Fielding's works and

Preface

to Dr. John Cadden and Thomas Hurley who patiently read the manuscript. I cannot overlook the help Donald Jensis gave me during my first interview with Mr. Fielding, nor can I end the list of those to whom I am indebted without mention of Dr. Paul Doyle who introduced me to Fielding's works. From that first introduction I read everything Fielding wrote until the conviction formed within me that I must write a book about an individual whose works so intrigued me. Dr. Doyle, though immersed in his own writing, encouraged me with words and with concrete help. For that help and encouragement, my gratitude is profound.

ALFRED BORRELLO

*Kingsborough Community College
of the City University of New York*

Contents

Chronology

1916 Gabriel Fielding born Gabriel Barnsley in Hexham, Northumberland, England.
1925- Secondary education at the now defunct Grange School
1929 in Eastbourne.
1929- St. Edward's School, Oxford.
1931
1933 Faircourt Academy, Eastbourne.
1934 Llangefni County School, Anglesey.
1935- Received bachelor of arts degree from Trinity College,
1939 Dublin, with prizes in anatomy and biology.
1939- Completed medical studies at St. George's Hospital
1942 Medical School, London; earned membership (1942) in the Royal College of Surgeons (England) and licentiate in the Royal College of Physicians (London).
1943 Married Edwina Eleanor Cook, October 31; began medical career as a lieutenant in the Royal Army Medical Corps.
1944 Commissioned a captain.
1946 Left the Royal Army Medical Corps.
1948 Began private practice in Maidstone, Kent, with two junior partners. Began his duties as a part-time medical officer in Her Majesty's Training Establishment (a prison) in Maidstone.
1952 First book published in England: *The Frog Prince and Other Poems*.
1954 *Brotherly Love* (published in America in 1961).
1955 *Twenty-Eight Poems* (published in England only).
1956 *In the Time of Greenbloom* (published in America in 1957).

1958 *Eight Days* (published in America in 1959).
1960 *Through Streets Broad and Narrow* (published in America in 1960).
1962 *The Birthday King* (published in America in 1963).
1963 Received the W.H. Smith Annual Award for *The Birthday King* as the most outstanding contribution to English Literature over a two-year period (1962-1963).
1964 Awarded the Thomas More Gold Medal for *The Birthday King*, cited as the most distinguished contribution to Catholic literature in 1963.
1966 *Gentlemen in Their Season* (published in America the same year). Currently writer in Residence, Washington State University, Pullman, Washington.
1967 Honorary Doctorate of Literature (Litt.D.), Gonzaga University, May 28.
1972 *New Queens for Old: A Novella and Nine Stories* (published in America the same year).

CHAPTER 1

In the Beginning

A writer, Gabriel Fielding once observed, takes, like seaweed, his texture from the atmosphere in which he finds himself. From his first moment of consciousness, he is unduly sensitive to family pressures. This sensitivity is the reason that the parents of writers always appear as so much larger-than-life characters. His brothers and sisters may think that they are living in a normal home, but the author *knows* he is in a dangerous jungle in which beasts stalk. An author's first book, Fielding noted, will probably be an attempt to wrest order, some pattern, from what appears to him to be "the pity and terror of life." When that first book appears, his relatives will be tempted to sue him for defamation of character, not realizing that it is a "most passionately loving attempt to put things right for them." When he has written this first book, his first pattern—that which Henry James calls "The Figure in the Carpet"—the writer will still be a "very damp piece of seaweed."

Eventually, however, the country and the times in which he is living, the currents of new ideas and discoveries and world news, will all be shedding their droplets into the atmosphere in which he is soaking. Before long, he is again obliged to turn to a theme from which he can pattern these new preoccupations. Nevertheless, despite their appeal, the pattern of his first book—the one he "forged out of the first terrors and loves of childhood"—will have much to do with the structure of his new story. And thus it will be with all that he writes. He will never entirely escape the events of his life, try as he might; for in these events he senses the patterns of all life.[1]

Thus, in describing the genesis of a novelist, Fielding described most accurately his own development. Born Alan Gabriel Barnsley in Hexham, Northumberland, March 25, 1916, Gabriel Fielding was the fifth of six surviving children of George Barnsley and Katherine Mary Fielding Smith Barnsley, both of whom, as well as his brothers and sisters (Derek, Godfrey, Mary, Michael), appear as characters in the Blaydon family trilogy. Fielding traces his ancestry to the brother of the novelist Henry Fielding through his maternal grandfather, Henry Fielding Smith, who was a minister. Like other members of the family, the grandfather, too, appears in *Brotherly Love* though not in the other volumes of the trilogy. Despite the family relationship, however, Fielding confesses that he had not read any of his ancestor's works, except his letters in his grandfather's possession, before he began his own career as a professional writer.

I *The Early Years*

George Barnsley, Fielding's father, was a relatively well-to-do clergyman of the Church of England—as is his fictional counterpart—whose health was adversely affected by his experiences as a soldier in World War I. While on duty in Italy, he had contracted sleeping sickness which afflicted him for the remainder of his life. The elder Barnsley remembered vividly and negatively his contacts during the war with Germans. Often he related these experiences to his family; and from them and those contacts with the German social attitude related by other members of his family, Fielding developed a life-long distrust of the German nation and its warlike proclivities. This distrust, bordering on horror, clearly manifests itself in the closing sections of *Through Streets Broad and Narrow*. *The Birthday King*, Fielding relates, probably owes its very existence to the gas mask, a wartime souvenir of his father with which he and his sister as children played. That gas mask figured in the stories which his father told. For Fielding it served as a symbol of the evil which motivates so many of the characters in that book.

Fielding's mother, who converted his father to high-church

Anglicanism, was a playwright, who wrote under the pen name of Katherine Mary Fielding. In this name Fielding dedicates *In the Time of Greenbloom* to her. In addition to writing plays, Mrs. Barnsley was a well-known breeder of Whippets; and one of these dogs, who resemble rather nervous greyhounds, appears in a scene in *Brotherly Love.* Something of Mrs. Barnsley's character can be glimpsed in the portrait her son draws of Mrs. Blaydon in his books. She had a strong psychic sense and, on numerous occasions, was uncannily aware of what was going on among her children and what would happen to those emotionally attached to her. Something of this sensitivity is woven into the character of John Blaydon as he appears in the trilogy, most particularly in a key scene in *In the Time of Greenbloom.* More significantly, this psychic, intuitive sense becomes part of the philosophical structure of Fielding's novels and a supporting point for the theories of human relationships which guide his development of character.

Mrs. Barnsley also exhibited a strong sense of righteousness which she imparted freely to her husband and her children. "From this scriptural righteousness," Fielding notes, "stemmed a whole network of exortations and prohibitions" from the tangle of which he has never been able to escape.[2] Like him, his fictional John Blaydon suffers from this rigid sense of right and wrong that has been given to him by his mother. And like his creator, a sense of sin where there is no sin, and of guilt where there is no real guilt, pursues him through the three volumes in which he appears.

Early in Fielding's life the family moved to Sussex and subsequently to Yorkshire, the setting of *In the Time of Greenbloom* and the book which inspired it in part, Emily Brontë's *Wuthering Heights.* Like the characters of the Brontë novel, which he confesses overpowered him, Fielding wandered in his youth over the moors and drank in the moodiness which that landscape intensifies in any individual of feeling. At the age of eight, he was sent to a "snob" preparatory school, the Grange School, Eastbourne. Like many of his fellow writers who had similar experiences, he found this a "terrible separation." He tells of the horrible and intense emotional pain he felt at being literally "ripped" from the comfort of his family and dragged into exile into the coldness of the boarding school. At that school, it seemed to him that everyone "from the masters to hens" was hostile. Nevertheless, he counts the experience as valuable to his art. "I think," he wrote, "that this, in a sense, was the beginning of the pain of which I write." Some of the experiences he had he incorporates into a chapter of *In the Time of Greenbloom.*

He received his public-school training at a Church of England school for the sons of the clergy, St. Edwards, Oxford, from 1929 to 1931. His experiences there were again not very pleasant. He vividly remembers being quite ill much of the time. These memories he also incorporates into John Blaydon's history. He notes that much of his introspection which was inherited, in part, from his mother dates from this period of his life when he found himself excluded from the group which usually controls the lives of students in the English public schools. He records that he became "extremely frightened of people." About his school experiences, he remarks, "Perhaps it was in that early period that I decided that I would one day use my pain and the insight it gave me in a career as a writer."[3] This belief that the early experiences of an individual shape his adult life finds expression in each of his novels but especially in the Blaydon family trilogy. There, John's emotional experiences with and attraction to Victoria *(In the Time of Greenbloom)* determine to a large extent the relationships he develops in *Through Streets Broad and Narrow.* In that novel, the painful memory of Victoria and her horrible death haunts his relationships with women.

Like John Blaydon, though not for the same reason, Fielding failed to pass his examinations and left St. Edwards (1931) and enrolled at Faircourt Academy, Eastbourne, for private tutoring. That academy closely parallels, even to the headmaster, the one in which John Blaydon was enrolled in *In the Time of Greenbloom.* Soon after, Fielding, again unsuccessful in his studies, entered the Llangefni County School on the Island of Anglesey, the family's home in Wales. Though embarrassed by the fact that he was older than most of the students in his class, he nevertheless remembered the school with warmth and fondness. He related that he witnessed in it the best teaching since he had first enrolled in school.

He decided, after much soul-searching and parental direction, to try his hand at medicine even though he most desired to "read English at Oxford." Two of his brothers were already there, but neither was doing well scholastically. Anxiously, his parents pressed medicine as a career by noting that so many doctors have become good writers—William M. Thackeray, Arthur Conan Doyle, Bram Stoker, and Somerset Maugham. They insisted that medicine would be a good discipline for him; moreover, if he failed at writing, which is what they thought would happen, he would not starve. He acquiesced, and in 1939 he took his bachelor of arts degree from Trinity College, Dublin, where he went "numbly, almost dumbly, through the medical course." While there, like his counterpart, John Blaydon, who also attended the school *(Through Streets Broad and Narrow)*, Fielding wrote a satiric paper for the Biological Association that criticized the Dublin hospitals, and its result was considerable difficulty in his finding admission to a hospital for his residency. He was finally admitted to St. George's Hospital, Hyde Park Corner; and he qualified there in 1942. He earned membership in the Royal College of Surgeons (England) and his licentiate in the Royal College of Physicians (London). His medical career began as a lieutenant in the Royal Army Medical Corps in 1943, the same year that he married Edwina Eleanor Cook.[4] His happiness, however, was clouded by the tragic death from a fall of his oldest brother, Derek, to whom he was attached. Much of this emotional attachment and the pain he suffered from his brother's death are recorded in his first novel *Brotherly Love* (1954).

Fielding left the Medical Corps as a captain in 1946 and settled with his wife into the life of a provincial doctor in Maidstone, Kent. Fielding was also, for a time, a prison doctor, as is the character Chance in *Eight Days*. During the course of Fielding's prison experience, he met and worked with the insane murderer who was to become the prototype of Marcovicz in that volume. The attachment Marcovicz shows for Dr. Chance is essentially the same as the con-

demned man's relationship with Fielding. His prison experiences were also used to a degree in *Gentlemen in Their
Season,* in which Coles is a "prison visitor" who meets a condemned man, Christopher, during his rounds. The character of Christopher also takes part of his being from
Fielding's encounters with the inmates.

II *His Career Begins: His Conversion*

In 1954, Fielding had an experience which he counts,
next to his marriage, as the most influential act in his life
as a writer: he became a convert to Catholicism after a life
of relative indifference to religion. Like John Blaydon, he
was during the first ten years of his life a Christian because
his parents were Christian. He had grown up in a household
similar to the one described in the Blaydon trilogy, a household filled with a ritualistic approach to faith. For years,
"faith" meant nothing more to him than adherence to the
outward manifestations of religion, the close attendance
upon which his mother insisted. After that period he "en-
dured a spell of twenty years when he was nothing"; indeed,
he was the "typical secular pagan of today" much like Coles
in *Gentlemen in Their Season.* Fielding turned his attention
to a fashionable reading of Buddhism and gradually became
very "left-wing" in his belief that all the ills of the world
were materialistic in origin. Soon he discovered that medicine, materialism, or, for that matter, Buddhism could not,
or did not, adequately explain his world or solve his personal
problems which, like those of all of his protagonists, were
looming larger in his life and threatening to inundate him.
He began to reinvestigate the Christianity of his youth and
ultimately, through a "passionate" reading of Graham Greene,
whom he deeply admired, and Evelyn Waugh, he examined
Roman Catholicism. His entry into the church resolved an
"enormous part" of his personal difficulties that had threatened to overwhelm him.[5]

But Catholicism assumed greater meaning over the years
in terms of his personal life and, most emphatically, of his
writing. That faith brought him into contact with the world
of Catholic thought and the philosophies of Gabriel Marcel,
the Christian Existentialist; Jacques Maritain; Ludwig Witt-

genstein; Martin Buber; and the writings of Medieval mystic
Juliana of Norwich, all of whom profoundly influenced the
substance of his writing. Fielding also credits his faith
with much of the control of his craft which his critics have
been quick to praise. He believes that, "without my conversion, I would have drifted off into much more complex,
undisciplined kinds of books in which there would have
been no sort of reference to a scale of values."[6]

More important to his art than his control over his craft,
he credits his conversion with presenting him with "the
meaning of life"—"I mean that secret inner thing inside
yourself of love and hate, hope and fear." This meaning
gives depth, scope, and breadth to his novels. Through this
understanding, he coolly and dispassionately writes of the
ever-present contradictions with which life is filled. When he
discovered that there existed a "great frame, a theological
frame of reference which satisfactorily explained these hidden battles within myself, I climbed aboard as if it were a
raft and I were a tired swimmer, and I rested; and there I
have rested ever since, but it has not been an idle rest. In
some ways the battle is sharper than it was before, but it's
on the battlefield whose definitions are drawn for me."[7]
He had longed to enter this battlefield and battle, essentially
the world of the professional writer, from the age of six
years. But only after his thirty-seventh birthday could he give
serious attention to his desire. He had to pay for the freedom
to write. His service as a doctor, he notes, was "the sentence
I had to fulfill in order to be free to write."[8]

He remembers with pleasure the years between 1922 and
1924, and his first thrilling encounters with the world of
literature. He and his sister had a nurse, Nanky Poo (who
appears in *Brotherly Love*), who habitually gathered the
two children, deposited them in a great armchair, and read
to them in the hour before bedtime. The stories she chose,
he recounts, held his attention more than the motion pictures
in the parish hall; for they held a particular power over him.
Through them, he seemed to achieve even impossible
dreams. The story that most fascinated him was a serial that
appeared in *Merry-Go-Round,* an upper-middle-class weekly
edited for children by Walter de la Mare. Essentially the

tale is about a small boy's discovery in a black thorn hedge
of an ebony wand which he used to attain all his desires.
That wand, Fielding indicated, represented the certainty
he had that he, too, should one day possess such a power.

The next step in his groping development as a writer
Fielding credits to the reading of a children's newspaper,
Chicks Own, which, because it was syllabified, made him
realize that he could eventually read a whole book by himself without the aid of his nurse. This great feat he accomplished at an early age while bedded by a childhood ailment. The book was a small, illustrated work by Beatrix
Potter. And when he had finished it, he became convinced
that he had achieved the wand of the earlier story. From that
point, he records, he was determined to "make stories"; for
he had discovered that for him, at least, the magic wand
was his pen.[9]

Immediately upon recovering from his illness, he went
to the small nursery bookshelf which contained some forty
volumes, from the Bible to Jonathan Swift's *Gulliver's Travels,*
and wrote his name in each, not to establish his ownership
but rather to suggest, in his imagination, that he had written
them all. The fact that he had not made no difference. This
conviction that he was to become a writer was soon forgotten
for most of the time for it was crowded out by the business
of growing up. The earlier experiences did, nevertheless,
leave their imprint. He notes that he could never go to the
cinema or read a story without pondering how he could im-
prove upon it or imitate it without being found out.

During this period of his youth, he had an increasing
awareness of the physical act of his mother's writing. He
recalls observing her with envy as she wrote dialogue which
he secretly believed he could never equal in merit. Yet,
interestingly enough, one of the aspects of his mature work
most appreciated by critics is his ability to create, as one
observes, "remarkable conversation."[10] His mother had been
writing plays since World War I and had staged many pieces:
children's plays, usually "patriotic and fantastic and a good
deal influenced by J. M. Barrie." In 1922, her greatest success, *The Great Big World,* was staged at the Court Theatre
by J. B. Fagan. This play, like all her plays in general, was

strongly moralistic in tone. A young family, very much resembling her own, have returned home for the Christmas holidays to be greeted on Christmas morning by Father Time who leads them into the great big world swarming with angels, tigers, and baboons.

Significantly, Fielding, in a conversation, recalled only *The Great Big World* and two other pieces of his mother's even though she had been writing for some thirty years. The significance lies essentially in the fact that his own work reflects something of these plays. One of these plays, *The Dove*, set in Yorkshire, resembles *In the Time of Greenbloom;* and, like that novel and *Eight Days* and *The Birthday King*, it concerns a world that conspires to crush the workings of the Holy Spirit in the heart of man. The other, *The Silken Purse* which is similar to *The Great Big World* and *The Dove* in its strong moralistic substructure, caught the attention of Sybil Thorndike, the actress; but it was never given a London production. A Welsh peasant boy of great intellectual promise is the protagonist of *The Silken Purse.* Despite his great potentialities, his struggle to escape the weakness of the flesh, embodied in an attractive but ignorant village girl, and the lackluster world in which he is slowly maturing is futile. Eventually, he is destroyed by that world and more significantly by his lust. Like the peasant boy, Fielding's protagonists struggle with their strong sexual desires and their societies to develop their potentialities. Their defeat comes when they realize that their desire for success in terms of their appetites and their societies is futile. Yet their defeat, paradoxically, marks the beginning of their victory.

In addition to the superficial parallels existing between his and his mother's work, the plays hold a different significance for Fielding. He records his jealousy of her activity and her "furious busyness," as well as her ability to develop believable dialogue. This jealousy was so great that he recalls frequently encouraging her in her work, believing "all the time that one day when I had discovered whatever it was I lacked, I would outshine her."[11] Despite his growing desire to become a writer and the attractions and the ultimate significance that his mother's work held for him, he did no writing whatsoever until he was sent to preparatory school in Eastbourne where the students were accustomed to write home each Monday. One of the teachers would list on the blackboard the "dreary" items of school business in order to help the boys to fill their letters with school news of the past week. Young Fielding often substituted items which transformed these missives into "truthful, catty, and boastful letters."

These letters were the extent of his creative efforts until a teacher began a competition for the best detective story, and the prize for the winner was a "shilling block of Cadbury's nut milk chocolate." Fielding set about to capture that prize with the aid of Michael McNeil, the son of "Sapper" Bulldog Drummond McNeil, who supplied the plot very much in the vein of those of his father's. Fielding won, but he was not terribly pleased because the story was not entirely his own even though the young McNeil had had no role in the actual writing. This displeasure prevented Fielding from making a second attempt at writing until his enrollment at public school.

There he began to work on his own version of *Beowulf*, which he had read in transtation. The choice is interesting in that it mirrors to some extent the ideal all of his characters cherish: that of the unblemished hero who triumphs over all adversity and, even in final defeat, meets a glorious end. But Fielding never proceeded very far into the work, nor with the original verse he was producing at ever-increasing intervals. He made futile attempts to have his poetry published in the school literary magazine; but as he puts it, "As with Kenneth Grahame, who had also been a pupil there, the school magazine rejected every contribution I ever submitted." Despite his lack of publication, his essays for his English classes were always praised; and he remembers his delight when they were sometimes read aloud by the instructor.

During this period of adolescence, he formed his secret desire to write professionally; but he had not yet determined the type of writing he was to do. He toyed with the idea of becoming an essayist, a poet, or playwright—all of which, except the last, he became. There seemed, however, one obstacle which lay between him and the novel: his

inability to construct a plot. Overriding this difficulty was
the simple hesitancy or uncertainty about undertaking the
enormous task of a "major" work. Nevertheless, despite
his fears, he knew that the task must be begun for even in
those days he was convinced that "whatever I ultimately
did would be 'outstanding.' "[12]

At Trinity College in Dublin, he began his first novel,
My Name Is Legion, which is, essentially, an attempt to
capture on paper his youth in Yorkshire. The story contained full sketches of his family as he had remembered
them. These characters later serve as the models of the
brothers, sisters, and parents of the later Blaydon trilogy.
When he had written some thirty thousand words, he sent
the manuscript to his eldest brother, Derek, who in turn,
forwarded it to a London publisher. The comments were
encouraging, but Fielding lost interest in completing it.
His emotions were then occupied with his medical studies,
which had become increasingly more onerous, and with a
long and unsatisfactory love affair with an Irish girl, who
is later the prototype of Dymphna in *Through Streets Broad
and Narrow.*

At this point, World War II seemed inevitable. That and
his search for a hospital in which to begin his residency
moved him with a strong desire to return to England. He
tried his hand at various short stories, but he invariably
abandoned them and turned to journalism and, during much
of 1941, wrote the "Londoner's Diary" column for the *London
Evening Standard.* He read voraciously during this period;
and each novel, third or first rate, suggested to him the pos-
sibility that, if he were sufficiently observant, he could discover the secret which so far had eluded him of constructing
a plot and a chronology out of which could emerge the real
story and emotion he wanted so desperately to convey.

His reading led him to the discovery of works which were
eventually to influence his own writing. He read Evelyn
Waugh, Graham Greene, Dostoevski, and Emily Brontë.
He recalls his first encounter years before with a Waugh
novel, *Vile Bodies.* His mother saw his father reading it much
to her horror, snatched it from his hands, and threw it into
the fire. Nevertheless, novels like *Vile Bodies* and other

early works of Waugh and Greene moved him deeply because of their "morbid gaiety." Fielding understood these
works as a refusal of their authors to be taken in "by the
sickness and obsessions of the century." Waugh's "wicked
wit" influenced Fielding the most and Greene's "earnestness
of search behind all the seedy, melodramatic happenings
of his characters."[13]

The death of his brother, Fielding's marriage, his mili-
tary service, and his postwar medical practice combined
for some years to deprive him of physical and emotional
time for writing. No opportunity to turn his full attention
to his writing occurred until he was confined to bed with
a duodenal ulcer of the type suffered by Dr. Chance in *Eight
Days*. He produced during this period *The Frog Prince*
(1952), his first collection of poetry, as well as the first draft
of *Brotherly Love*. He had difficulty finding a publisher
for *The Frog Prince* until he saw an article by Stephen
Spender about private publishers. When he wrote to Spender
of his dilemma, Spender suggested that he contact Erica
Marx who ran the Hand and Flower Press in Kent. Fielding
submitted the manuscript, which was accepted for publication. He sent a copy of *The Frog Prince* to Graham Greene;
and elated by the quality of the praise it received, he had
renewed hope that he would achieve success in writing.

Curtis Brown and Jonathan Cape, however, rejected
Brotherly Love. The rejection brought with it a discourage-
ment which forced Fielding to abandon prose for verse for
the next two years. The poems he produced during this
period later appeared in his second collection of poetry,
Twenty-Eight Poems (1955), again published by the Hand
and Flower Press. By 1953, however, he decided to resur-
rect *Brotherly Love*, completely rewrite it, and cast it in
the form of ten short stories. Hutchinson accepted the novel
on the basis of only three "chapters." Its publication in
England (1954) was relatively unnoticed; but eventually,
because of Graham Greene's interest and Evelyn Waugh's
"fascinated" distaste, the collection received some critical
acclaim. The quality of this notice supplied Fielding with the
impetus to begin his second novel, *In the Time of Greenbloom* (Hutchinson, 1956; Morrow, 1957). The book, in

turn, was received with glowing reviews, and these confirmed his desire to continue with his career.

Eight Days followed (published by Hutchinson in 1958 and Morrow in 1959), and Fielding returned to the Blaydon family for the third and last time in *Through Streets Broad and Narrow* (Hutchinson, 1960; Morrow, 1960). This novel was followed by *The Birthday King,* for which Fielding was awarded the prestigious W. H. Smith and Son Annual Award for the most outstanding contribution to English literature over a two-year period and the Thomas More Medal for the most distinguished contribution to Catholic literature in 1963.

During the period in which he produced the major part of his work, he turned his hand to the production of short stories and essays, many of the latter commenting directly upon his art in particular and the art of the novel in general. He was commissioned to prepare a cinematic treatment of Queen Nefertiti which took him to Egypt for background material, but the motion picture was never produced. But the trip far from fruitless, presented him with the background for the novel upon which he is presently at work.

In recent years, Fielding has concerned himself increasingly with the clarification of the direction his art is to take. In 1967, when he was asked to address the 36th Annual Shakespeare Birthday Program and Award Dinner of the Friends of Literature in Chicago, his address, "The Need for a Proper Evil," discussed his understanding of his own and his fellow novelists' art. In 1966, he accepted a position as Artist in Residence at Washington State University in Pullman, Washington, where he has remained as a professor of English. His lectures and his writings there are moving him toward a sharper understanding of the depths of his art which began with a reworking of the elements of his own life; and it appears that, in the usual almost organic way of genuine writers, he will continue to develop and portray other but less personal universal truths.

CHAPTER 2

The Most Important Part
of Living Is Loving

I *Early Works: Poetry*

EVERY novelist, consciously or unconsciously, develops out of the depths of his artistic sensibilities, his
observations, and his experiences an understanding of mankind and its place in the world which directs and shapes
those worlds created within the covers of his books. Generally, that understanding ultimately embraces man in
terms of his aspirations, his relationships to himself and to
others, and to the meaning of life. Often, the understanding directly affects the techniques the artist chooses to apply
in the creation of his works; and more often than not, this
understanding broadens and deepens in proportion to his
ability to sense, observe, and experience that life of which
he is a part and out of which he tailors the fabrics of his
imagination. Often this understanding exists rudimentarily
in the writer's early works and can be traced as it grows
deeper and stronger as the individual becomes more profi-
cient in his craft.

Such is the case with Gabriel Fielding. Like many authors
who look with distaste upon the works of their apprentice-
ship, he speaks critically of the poems he produced in his
first attempts at authorship. Though not pleasing to their
author, Fielding recognizes and notes the important relationship which exists between this verse, flawed though it
may be, and the bulk of his writing. He once stated, "I write
poems for the same reason I write prose: to try to pin down
in words some past event which still excites me."[1] Those
past events which excite him to write are the incidents

[28]

which reveal to him the fundamental patterns that support life as he comprehends it. Each incident presents that life, centered on man, as a rich and varied tapestry of ironies and contradictions which spring from man's essential struggle to achieve an emotional balance through a compromise between his ideals and the harsh realities of life. Fielding maintains that this struggle, essentially tragic yet strangely comic, is evident in all of man's emotions but most clearly and most poignantly in that human emotion which is common and so important to all: love. He holds that "the most important part of living is loving."[2] In the realm of love man most clearly confronts the dichotomy between his ideal and the reality with which he must live; and the confrontation shifts in dimension from the tragic to the comic in proportion to the involvement of the individual. The more involved he is, the more tragic the confrontation; the less involved, the more comic the affair becomes.

Through no accident, therefore, the first of Fielding's published poems and the bulk of his published verse concern love and its seriocomic implications. Practically all of his verse (forty-seven poems) is contained in two slim volumes, the first of which, *The Frog Prince and Other Poems* (1952), bears the name Alan Barnsley, for he was not to adopt his pen name of Fielding until the publication of *Brotherly Love*, his first novel. *The Frog Prince* contains some nineteen poems; the remainder are in *Twenty-Eight Poems* (1955); and neither of these volumes has an American edition. The title poem in Fielding's first collection, "The Frog Prince; Variations on a Theme," is particularly significant in tracing the development of his growing understanding of man. The poem reflects, in addition, many of those techniques he later perfects and applies in the creation of his novels; and this technique forces involvement on the part of the reader because it evokes memories common to the experience of all.

In "The Frog Prince," which was admired and praised by Graham Greene, Fielding conjures the memory of the fairy tale in which a handsome prince runs foul of the evil machinations of a wicked witch who turns him into an ugly frog. In the original tale, though a frog in body, he remains a prince in spirit with all his sensibilities and desires intact. Locked in the prison of his frustrations, only the freely given love of a beautiful princess can restore him to what he once was. Tragic, unspeakable, and unfulfillable as this condition is in reality, it is not impossible in the world of make-believe. The love is given, and the story ends with the heartening conclusion that the two will live happily ever after and reign over their kingdom.

Fielding takes this tale so dear to youth and so suitable to its unbounded optimism and faith in the future and reprojects it in terms of realistic maturity when most, if not all, of the illusions of youth have worn thin to reveal the basic frustrations which are the warp and woof of love and of life. To accomplish his objective, he presents the frog prince, whom the persona is schooling in the realities of life. Like the prince of the fairy tale, some evil force has trapped a noble spirit in the body of a frog. The force, in this instance, is not a witch but the physical fact of his birth into a world in which things can never be as he wishes them to be. The frog prince of the poem, like his counterpart in the fairy tale, "wears yet a precious jewel in his head," his dream of an ideal love, his inner vision of perfection. But unlike his counterpart, Fielding's frog prince will always remain what he is. His problems will not resolve themselves in the wish-fulfillment of childhood, and this truth he must learn.

Even the object of his desire, his princess, is flawed: "For you Green Prince there is/no house of gingerbread/your princess has migraine." Like her prince, she too dreams; but she, like him after he learns the painful lessons reality has to teach, "will forget/ There ever was a Prince or words/ of incantation in the wood." The voice of reality in guise of the persona tells her that she must not look to frog princes for her fulfillment. Instead she must look to men of flesh and blood who "will bring . . . painted/skins, a cup of strange design,/Bright mantles laced with feathers/And firkins of rare wine." She cannot, however, expect that these men of the real world will be handsome, young and strong; they will not possess these qualities which she, in her youthful aspirations, dreamed her lover would have. Though they may be old, "passion shakes their/Fingers just

the same." But taking an old man as a lover has compensa-
tions, not the least of which is the wealth he can bestow
with which "one hires a garden boy." But care must be tak-
en lest the old one suspect betrayal; she must remember
that "A shouldered leaf may mean you stood,/ But pollen
means you fell." The ultimate consolation, however, lies in
the knowledge that "one storm will fell the hollow elm."
Freedom and wealth are the rewards for patience.

As for the frog prince who yearns for his princess; he, too,
will finally "forget/there ever was a witch or words/of incantation in the wood." He will take into himself a lady like
himself whom he will rescue "with a tongue flick" from the
onslaught of the "dragonflies." And ultimately, he will take
possession of his "half an ell of ditch." That marshy world
over which he will preside, ironically analogous to the kingdom in the fairy tale, will echo with the valor of his deeds
even though they be small and, in terms of his dreams, in-
significant. Yet men of lesser strength and of lesser accomplishments will proclaim his greatness "and sweetly make it
known to men/the tongue's more mighty than the Fen." But
what a disappointment his reign will be in terms of his
dream, that "precious jewel in his head."

This disappointment is the key to an understanding of
Fielding's theme in the poem and, with variations, to the
themes in each of his novels. The sweet, richly optimistic
hope of youth in love and in its ultimate and absolute fulfillment is betrayed by the reality which is the product of
maturity; for things are never, nor can be ever, as one hopes
they will be. The lover, ironically, though he sets his sights
upon possession of a beautiful princess, ultimately and
willingly settles for a reptile like himself and will be, in
double comic irony, content with the settlement.

What Fielding projects in the poems is not a desire to reverse this condition, but, that this solution is the way of the
world as he sees it. He does not offer a remedy; he supplies,
rather, a diagnosis. He chooses love as the focus for that
diagnosis because it is the one emotion comprehendible by
all. In revealing the paradoxes implicit in the word "love,"
the source of life, he uncovers the larger paradox and ultimately the tragic-comic irony which is life. Man's aspira-

tions, lofty or limited as the frog prince's, are never fulfilled
precisely as he dreams of them; for these dreams are comic
in their dimensions. Compromise is necessary; and compromise implies, essentially, a betrayal of those aspirations
because the compromise demands that the individual
equate and finally identify them with attainable reality.
When the compromises and the adjustments have been
made, man's vision narrows; and he accepts the lesser
achievement for the greater. For the male, however, the
adjustment is difficult; and it must be couched in more acceptable, less direct terminology. Man is essentially the
"Green Prince" of the poem because he does not season
—mature—so easily as the female of the species. He is
more romantic and, therefore, less capable of compromise.
When maturity speaks to him in the voice of the persona, he
speaks in hidden, suggestive language of the compromises
he must make: "Be still, be still that/ In this moment may be
beauty,/ colors of the blown gown! Residing in the word or
whisper/ And the pause which follows it." The soothing
voice is not necessary for the female, for, though her aspirations parallel the male's, she is more readily capable of adjustment to the realities of life; hence, the persona, who
speaks to her more directly, reveals to a larger degree the
cynicism and hypocrisy which are essential ingredients of
adulthood. She should accept the embrace of age rather
than youth, for youth does not have the power to bestow
upon her the comforts of life. She can, nevertheless, enjoy a youthful lover if she takes care to conceal her actions
from her old love. Ultimately, if patient, she will possess
the wealth of her aged love and yet be young enough to
enjoy life.

Fielding's picture of the processes of maturation contains
a sadness. In achieving adulthood, the individual loses
the innocence of youth, which, attractive though it may
be, is not suitable for life; yet, in achieving that maturity
he loses even more for he must accept a fundamentally
hypocritical life style. This irony of maturation is considered again and again in each of Fielding's novels, but it is
most poignantly present in *The Birthday King* and in each
volume of the Blaydon trilogy. "Alfried's Angels" are like

the frog prince's; dream-princess, and other aspects of this poem suggest additional devices of style that Fielding employs in his prose. Significantly, the chief of these devices is revealed in the subtitle of the work, "Variations on a theme." Fielding focuses on a single theme: love in this poem and in each of his novels; and like a musician, he examines its several variations and produces a totality of effect. He moves through his theme first by focusing on love in terms of the romanticism of youth as exemplified by the "Green Prince" who apprehends his love in terms of idealistic wish-fulfillment. Then Fielding turns to an examination of love not only in terms of reality but in those of the female of the species. Finally, he returns to a reconsideration of the frog prince, who, now seen in the light of his "marshy world," is no longer the romantic lover but one who has focused his aspirations on the attainable reality. This shifting from viewpoint to viewpoint suggests a development of the central theme, as well as the nature of the figures upon whom the persona focuses his attention. This device is especially effective when Fielding develops the character of John Blaydon in his first novel, *Brotherly Love*, as well as in the two subsequent novels in his trilogy.

Yet another device Fielding employs later is reflected in his treatment of the frog prince. He ostensibly offers a frog—a rather comic figure in his repulsiveness yet one like all lovers as they see themselves in the eyes of the beloved—to play the idealistic lover; but hidden beneath its skin, is a prince with "a precious jewel in his head"—a lover sensitive, romantic, attuned to the ideal. Like his characters in his novels, the surface picture does not reveal the actuality; nor can it, for Fielding operates, as his treatment of the theme in this poem suggests, in a world in which things are not truly what they appear to be on the surface. A recognition of this fact leads to the development of the paradoxes and the subsequent ironies that weave beneath the surface of this poem and all of his work, not the least of which is implicit in the state of the frog—a creature so ugly yet so desirous of the beauty which he cannot, ironically, possess on his own terms. The pool wherein he resides, in terms of his seeking for that love which will truly fulfill his longing, must "be broken and made whole." The "breaking" also suggests a "breaking" with the dream, for only in its destruction can "wholeness" be achieved. The paradox is presented in the physical image of a frog leaping out of the water, breaking its surface, and returning to its depths—and the agitation of that surface is replaced by the calm smoothness of still water.

Like the frog prince, so the princess is also caught in a web of paradoxes. The persona calls her his daughter. Yet, before presenting her with his "advice," he assumes that she, like her male counterpart, is possessed by that "incantation in the wood"—the romantic vision of what her life will or should become. As has been noted, his advice is a mass of paradoxes: she is to offer her love to an old man; but this "love" is not truly love, the love she would offer to the man of her dreams. The persona tells her to give of herself; but the giving, like the loving, is bound by a price: there is no giving in this instance; there is only a selling. Maturity suggests that love is not the total and complete involvement of the romantics but a retention of all that can be retained and the "giving" of oneself occurs only when it cannot be avoided. The persona advises the princess that the old man be "teased" with "the croissants when you need an afternoon." Under this ironic banner, maturity parades its understanding of love; but it seems to forget that love is placing the loved one "far inside [one's] secret self," a melding of two into one personality, into a new being.

In giving such cynical advice, the persona, maturity, establishes a tension in the poem which is never lost in each of Fielding's novels. Maturity suggests that form and surface only be observed; youth demands emotional honesty despite the surface appearance. This dichotomy is reflected in the very structure of the poem. On first reading, it suggests a tightly structured unity, divided as it is into three sections with an obvious, rather rigidly controlled movement from section to section and dominated by a refrain repeated with only slight variation from section to section. Yet, in the midst of the tight structure, resides the freedom of the lines.

When the frog prince is first addressed, the lines are as loose, as formless, and as free as his romantic dreams; and so, too, at first, are the lines of the persona's advice to the princess. But as his proscriptions to her grow more rigid, rhyme creeps in to suggest rigidity. Finally, in the third and last section, as the frog prince assumes his place in the world of reality, the poem ends in a series of three sestets rhymed *abac dd,* and the final couplet in each sestet suggests the rounded sense of mature reason that is gaining final and irrevocable control over the romantic formlessness of the previous stanzas.

The closing rigidity of these final stanzas is also paradoxical in the light of the nature imagery employed throughout the poem and most strongly in the last section. The reader is treated to rich and clear pictures of an English wood and of the insects that inhabit it. There are the dragonflies "who rain their fires/from every bright vermilion scale/" and whose veined wings resemble lyres, and the pool is a gathering of "liquid fragments in a bowl." In addition to serving as a paradoxical motif in terms of the rigidity of the structure, Fielding's use of nature imagery calls to mind yet another device he frequently employs in other of his poems as well as in his novels: he takes aspects of the familiar past—bits of literature, history, as in *The Birthday King,* or nursery rhymes—and through a slight refocusing, reprojects them into a contemporary framework. In this framework, they suggest by indirection Fielding's understanding of man and his condition. Thus, in the poem under consideration, Fielding's references to the young lady who is counseled to wed an older man evokes Chaucer's "Miller's Tale" in which January and May are united much to January's consternation and to the reader's edification. The total effect achieved with this allusion is one of tragic comedy; for the reader cannot but sense the serious aspects of such a match, nor can he overlook the humor implicit in it.

In another poem ("Eve"), Fielding uses Genesis to supply him with a similar framework on which to project his point. The poet discovers "Eve" among "the mill girls/ clad in shawls/With Woolworth pearls/ About her throat."

As he contemplates this contemporary Eve, he concludes
that she, with her garage-hand Adam whom she will "wed
at week-end," cannot and will not "guess/the bitterness
she must endure/ As breeding dulls her tinsel face/ And
years annul her promised grace." Here again, Fielding
underscores the paradox of love. Just as the frog prince and
his frog princess must settle for less than their dreams, so
must Eve and her Adam eventually accept not the living
"happily ever after" of their aspirations but, in fulfillment
fo their love, a sapping of their beauty. Fulfillment, Fielding seems to say, destroys the dream.

In "Novitiate," which is suggestive of the Wordsworth
sonnet "Nuns Fret Not at Their Convent's Narrow Room,"
Fielding stresses yet another paradox that he senses to be
implicit in life. The life of the Nun, willingly accepted, is
less constraining and less dehumanizing than that of life in
the mature world outside the convent walls. Death, too, he
finds paradoxical; for in probing its dimensions in "The
Lodger," he discovers that in reality death is "a stillness
more familiar than sleep." And rather than marking the end
of maturity, Fielding regards death as a "bestower of an
infancy," thereby suggesting it to be the moment of entry
into a new life. Death is a return to the innocence of birth.

Fielding returns to the world of childhood innocence in
"Jack and Jill," "Jack Horner" and "Bo Peep." Like "The
Frog Prince," these poems are evocative of the nursery
rhymes known and remembered by all; and as in that poem,
Fielding uses them to underscore the irony implicit in maturation. Jack and Jill, portrayed long after the fall, suggest
the fall of Adam and Eve from grace and the loss of childhood innocence. Jack achieves a measure of ease from his
pain by dwelling on the somewhat less than comforting
knowledge that he and Jill can "never . . . go back down
the visiting lane." Jill knows "he'll never bear again the
brimming pail." Like the princess in "The Frog Prince,"
she is the stronger of the two; and she will comfort her Jack
even though she also has pain: "She'll comfort him . . ./
And tell no soul her sorrows/ Nor stop the adder from his
laughter/ That she, the first to fall, should tumble after."

Like Jack and Jill, "Jack Horner" has a lesson to teach

about innocence and maturity. In identifying his virtue, Jack Horner destroys the value of his being "a good boy." His declaration of pride in himself is his first mature act. And Bo Peep does wrong in worrying over the sheep: "Why call them back who wandered from her dream/ . . . soon enough they must return from some fat fold." Their innocent straying will soon come to and end, and they will return to the control of their master. The sheep suggest the same type of innocence possessed by the Frog Prince, Eve, Jack and Jill, and the other characters in Fielding's poetry before they begin their descent into the maelstrom of maturity.

II Brotherly Love

Fielding's concern with the innocence of childhood and its paradoxical seriocomic relationship to maturity that is projected in these poems continued and was deepened and broadened in *Brotherly Love*. Though his first novel to be published in England (1954), it was his third to be circulated in America after the critical success of *In the Time of Greenbloom* (his second novel and the second volume of the Blaydon trilogy) and *Eight Days* (not part of the trilogy). Graham Greene, to whom Fielding had sent a copy, wrote that *Brotherly Love* was "an extraordinarily good beginning." Evelyn Waugh, on the other hand, while praising the book for being "well conceived and executed," found it fundamentally "unpleasant" because of Fielding's treatment of Anglicanism and the Anglican clergy.

Essentially, *Brotherly Love* is episodic in structure; it consists of ten chapters—in reality ten short stories and originally composed as such—which trace dramatic events in the life of an Anglican clergyman's family. These ten chapters cluster in three parts which are roughly suggestive of the three divisions of "The Frog Prince": "Northumberland," "The Island of Anglesey," and "Kent." The second part consists of a single chapter, "Brotherly Love," which serves structurally as the pivot on which the plot and, most significantly, the theme hinge. "Northumberland," which focuses on the family's youth and specifically on John Blaydon's childhood, reveals the relative emotional remoteness which exists, because of the difference in their ages, between him and his brother David whom he idolizes. "The Island of Anglesey" brings the brothers together for a confrontation, a clarification, and redefinition of their relationship. The final section, "Kent," draws them apart once again; but their relationship because of their remoteness is essentially different from that which is the result of John's immaturity in the first section.

That first section also reflects a significant remoteness of locale when contrasted with the third one. Northumberland is as relatively unsophisticated as the young Blaydon family who live in it. Kent, on the other hand, as one of the home counties contiguous with London, suggests ironically that the family has grown older and more sophisticated but no wiser in its interrelationships. The essential pattern of these relationships develops in the first chapter of Part I, "In the Beginning." The title is ironic, just as the closing words of the volume are: "the end of the beginning." There is no ending and no beginning here, merely a continuation, a flowing and merging of one generation into another. The construction of events depicted in the chapter implies this continuation when, through them, the reader is introduced to characters who represent three generations of the family: John and his brother David, Mr. and Mrs. Blaydon, but most important, the maternal grandfather whom the children call Pall Mall. He resembles David closely; and, like David who is to become one, he is an Anglican Priest; a product of the late Victorian and Edwardian periods, he is proper and reserved on the surface but tainted with a long history of illicit sexual adventures. Hints are whispered about "trouble" with the maids; and John, though uncomprehending because of his youth, is witness to his grandfather's interest in Nanny. Mrs. Blaydon fears that David will someday be very much like her father. She loves him as she loves her son, yet the fear she feels permeates her relationships to them and the very atmosphere of the book. This fear is the source of the sense of guilt that mars even the happiest of events and the love the children have for one another.

Because of the seriocomic incident upon which this

chapter is built, it has greater structural significance, however, than the introduction of the principal characters. When John, in childish and unthinking playfulness, jumps at his grandfather as he is descending the staircase, the old man falls down the three flights of stairs which lead from the nursery, carrying his grandchild with him. When the pair arrive at the bottom, the comic picture of intertwined arms, twisted bodies, and broken dignity quickly changes to tragedy when John believes that he has killed his beloved Pall Mall. Even when his grandfather revives, John's sense of guilt clings to him. The full ironic implications of the incident are revealed in Part III, when David, who has indeed turned out in every way to resemble his grandfather, dies in a fall while practicing with John for a mountain-climbing expedition. Once again John's sense of guilt is deepened.

Thus, Fielding frames his tale in death, some form of death; for physical or spiritual or emotional death is present in each of the chapters. Death becomes the warp upon which he weaves the somewhat complicated themes of the novel. These themes, in turn, are projected and refined in the remaining novels in the trilogy.

Death also gives another dimension to the story: it removes the tale from the narrow confines of a single family and broadens it until it becomes a metaphor for life as Fielding understands it: life is rounded by death. In terms of death and its awful implications for mankind, nothing, not even faults of character or the sin which Mrs. Blaydon fears so much, is of any great consequence. When David dies, John is only, and can only be, concerned with the state of his brother's soul as it begins its long journey through eternity.

Brotherly Love covers the most extensive period of time in the life of John Blaydon, the central figure of the trilogy, who is first presented as a child of eight. When David dies, John is at the threshold of maturity. Unlike the other two novels, however, this one appears to be focused on David, the oldest brother, the first of the Blaydon children and the idol of his mother. The American advertisements for the book claimed that the novel is David's, not John's; but this claim is essentially a misreading of the novel. John, the youngest son, has a close love and affinity for David insofar as David serves as the model for his life instead of the father, who, though loving, is essentially ineffectual in directing his children. Because control and direction of the boys is in the hands of the mother, Mrs. Blaydon, David becomes a father-figure for John; and David's presence, in the child's mind, represents stability. In David's hands lies the solution to the countless problems which beset the family. But David, when the reader first meets him, is the central figure in a struggle for control of his own identity. The struggle is waged against his mother and the smothering love she has for him. John is caught up with and becomes emotionally part of that struggle though seemingly a noncombatant.

This struggle for identity becomes one of the central themes of the novel. When Mrs. Blaydon firmly and finally decides that David, like her husband Edward and her father, must become an Anglican priest, she overlooks David's nature and proclivities and substitutes the traditions and forms and the surface conformity which control her own life and the lives of her family before her. Paradoxically, her decision also grows out of her love for him; for she genuinely believes that the path she has chosen for him is the correct path, the only path he can take. Just as paradoxically, David's rebellion is developed in the context of his love for her. Their love leads to periods of tenderness during which the household is filled with apparent calm and peace; but more often than not, these periods are followed by storms of disobedience and independence. All the children suffer, but most of all John, who cannot comprehend the reason for his brother's rebellion. Why doesn't David give in, he asks himself?

In the light of John's emotional involvement, the struggle takes on larger proportions until it is, essentially, one between the older and the younger generations. The struggle is between the past, whose forms and rituals attempt to structure all life, and the present, which, desperate in its desire to resist the strictures imposed on it by the past, is without any genuine patterns of its own to apply. Evelyn Cavallo—who sees this struggle as peculiar to the British, especially in clerical families—classifies it as it appears in Fielding's book as the "revolt against the vicarage ethos."[4]

But the struggle is more than the battle of opposing wills, for it has wider application than to the British clergy. Another dimension is the attempt, founded upon love, of the older generation—the past, so to speak—to guard, guide, and protect the young; to warn them of impending danger. The irony implicit in this desire is evident in life. There is no resolution to the problems that beset each generation when its role changes from the guided to the guider, or from the protected to the protector, just as there is no resolution to *Brotherly Love.*

David conforms, apparently, to his mother's wishes by becoming an Anglican priest. Yet his conformity is confined only to the surface, for he remains the essential David. His sexual appetite grows rather than diminishes; and his restlessness, his charm, all are there beneath the black cassock, even his proclivity for mountain climbing remains intact. This proclivity, suggestive of all of his interests and of his character, leads to his death. But David's death resolves nothing. John, at that juncture, is caught up in the selfsame problems of identity with similar dimensions. Love is also the focus of his difficulties. He senses that he cannot find himself unless he finds love, but the need is not for the love of his mother which had once satisfied him and been all consuming. Like the frog prince, like David, John seeks love in its romantic ideal; and like them, he is frustrated by reality.

John is shy and backward in his lovemaking. One summer, his emotions fix on a young French girl, Giselle, who is living close to the family's home on the Island of Anglesey. The epitome of his dreams of romantic love, she is beautiful, intriguing, knowledgeable, foreign. He feels awkward in her presence, crude, unpolished. David, at this point in the story, receives orders in the Church and is married; and he comes with his wife to visit the family. When the women—David's mother, wife, and sister—go one day to shop in the village and leave David, John, and Giselle to fend for themselves, they decide to go fishing. John is insensitive, at first, to David's interest in the girl and to her growing fascination for him. He discovers their mutual interest only too late. The two leave him on some pretext and go off by themselves. When they fail to return, John's fears that David has embarked upon another affair are confirmed. Torn by his jealousy and the new dimension it has given his relationship with his brother—now not only a brother but a rival in love—and loyal to the fraternal love he still has for him, John tries desperately to hide what is transpiring from the women who have returned from their shopping; but his subterfuge is unsuccessful. The women are profoundly disturbed by David's actions, but even more moved is John.

John's admiration for his brother diminishes, and David is no longer the idol to be admired and emulated. Besides anger and wounded masculine pride, John has come more importantly to realize the depths of his brother's sexual hunger. He is appalled and repelled by it; but significantly, he instinctively recognizes in himself the birth of a similar hunger. Once only sympathetic to his brother's emotional turmoil, he now feels an awakening empathy. Ironically, and somewhat comically, that empathy forges an even stronger bond between the brothers than John's earlier admiration: the cuckold loves the cuckolder even more firmly. This development suggests an element of deep import in Fielding's understanding of the human heart.

Once, when questioned about his creation of character, Fielding replied:

If you take Martin Buber and his I-Thou relationship, his theories persuade us that God is brought into the world by the total involvement of one person with another; by the sort of love which will know how the other person feels and thinks. I am not quite sure that it is God Who is brought into the world by novelists like me, but for me characters grow out of my complete involvement and sympathy with some person whom I invade with myself. Too often this means the deep exploration of the "shadow side."[5]

John's discovery of David's "shadow side" permits him to advance to a true understanding of his brother and to a truer, more genuine love for him than that marked by the idolatry of the past. With that development, David springs to life for John; for he is no longer the distant, somewhat out-of-

focus ideal he was when John was younger and less perceptive. Moreover, he is no longer regarded by John as the
tower of strength and as the possesser of all knowledge.
David, in his affair with Giselle, is infinitely more alive and
infinitely more real; his faults vivify him. Fielding, in suggesting that true existence flows only through the total involvement of one individual in another, is saying nothing
new. But when he adds another dimension to the concept,
he reveals something fresh about the process. This "shadow
side" to which he refers is that new dimension; for, when
one man approaches another in terms of weaknesses, a
mutual involvement is more easily accomplished. Understanding, sympathy, and love grow out of an awareness, not
of accomplishments but of failings. Mankind, Fielding
seemingly suggests, is limited not so much in the good it
can achieve but rather in the evil it perpetrates; but from
this evil good can flow. The guilt, the sins, and the failings
of man reveal his humanity; and in this revelation and understanding, ironically, lies man's greatest strength because
it breeds a sense of mutuality. More significantly, this revelation gives men an understanding of their dependent relationship to their Creator Who is perfection. Thus, the evil
in man sinks to insignificance when put to proper use and
viewed in proper perspective. Sin and guilt and longings
for what man should not possess are, paradoxically, not only
his greatest weakness but also the source of his greatest
glory.

When this belief is projected against Fielding's religious
sensibilities, it assumes greater meaning. Christ came into
the world because of man's weakness; and without human
evil, the world could not possess its Savior. In that sense,
man's proclivity to do evil is, ironically, his greatest gift,
since it can be made to lead to man's ultimate salvation. More
important in an earthly sense, the recognition of one's own
guilt and of sin in another can lead to a truer and firmer
brotherhood of man. Men are brothers because of their
mutual weakness and need for each other.

It is interesting that Fielding should have charged the
brothers, David and John, with the responsibility of carrying his understanding of mankind's plight. John is an ado-

lescent grasping desperately for maturity through his love for a girl relatively indifferent to him; David, a clergyman bound to the responsibilities of that state yet drowning in the depths of his sexuality. Through the situations that confront these brothers, Fielding focuses upon yet another facet of man's paradoxical position in this life; for reared in a household in which the formalities and prohibitions of faith were rigidly followed, the young men are continually torn between their ideals and their natural desires. Taught that a sinless perfection is their only goal, they are never given insight into and understanding of the failures they are inevitably to encounter because of their human imperfections. Their faith taught them to see sin everywhere in everything and, for them, faith became the center of their attention.

This sin-oriented, negative interpretation of faith presents an ever-growing problem to John as the novel develops, and the problem intensifies in the two remaining volumes of the trilogy. John begins to question the faith into which he was born. Like the older members of his family, John has been exposed from the first moment of his conscious life to the forms and formulas of belief. His first memories are of the round of prayers and rituals that regulate each day and that nothing interrupts. This rigid application to surface acts of faith causes the essential core of truths in that faith to grow stale and meaningless for John as he matures. On rare occasions, nevertheless, the true power of belief shines through, as in the case of his stricken sister.

Mary, John's older sister, is dying; and the family, torn with grief, prays for her in its accustomed manner with appropriate words and gestures, but to no avail. In desperation, Mrs. Blaydon insists that Father O'Brien, an Anglican priest especially noted for his sanctity, be summoned to administer the last rites of the church. Mary's room is prepared for his coming with the crucifix, candles, prie-dieu; and the family arranges itself about the room in the places customary for family worship. Father O'Brien prays silently for several minutes, then begins to anoint the dying girl with holy oils. Suddenly, the tone of his prayers changes; he no longer uses the reverent, somewhat obsequious tone with which John is familiar, having heard it used so often

and so ineffectively by his parents. Father O'Brien pronounces his prayers "as though he were demanding of someone something that was his by right; as though all was
prepared and made ready and he was calling impatiently on
someone who had promised to come and telling him that
he must hurry" (36).

John, strangely moved, senses in Father O'Brien's prayers
a power not contained nor reflected in the ritual of his parents.
Mary coughs, stirs, and shows signs that the crisis has passed;
and the family, relieved, returns to the dining room to discuss what has happened. John, however, sensitive to the
great event which he has witnessed—the direct power of
faith—cannot take part: he is content with his emotional
apprehension of the mystery of that power. On the other
hand, as a child, he knows that "grownups could never
leave things alone, never accept things without examination,"
and he silently leaves the room: "He felt as though he car-
ried a bright and fragile bowl in his arms, something so
costly and personal that he must bring it to his room untouched and unseen by anyone save himself" (38).

This early experience of John's with the power of faith
serves to confuse rather than clarify his relationship to it
as he matures. This confusion deepens as the years pass
until the paradox that is faith reveals itself to him. Mrs.
Blaydon, who believes so strongly and desperately in that
faith, uses it unknowingly to destroy the child she loves
the most, her beloved David, by forcing him into the life
for which he is not suited. She forces her family to adhere
to the round of prayers that grow ever more meaningless
and emptier as the children grow older:

Prayers in the summer when the sound from the garden seemed
suddenly to have been switched on like a wireless set; prayers
in the dark winter's mornings when everyone tried to kneel nearer
the fire, and prayers at night when the owls left the elms at Beddington. All these prayers down the years, and what have they
achieved? What single blessed happening in the light of the new
sun that was upon the century, had ever originated in them?

They had prayed for peace and there was war. They had prayed
for father's health and it was broken; they had prayed without
cease for the churches, and they were empty; they had prayed for

David and he was lost to them. Yet still they prayed, and would go on praying. Unless there was belief there could be no departure from it, and where there was no point of departure there could be no journey, no purpose in living and no return to Faith. They would become like the countless thousands lost in the cities, in the plains, in the great unmapped geography of the twentieth century, moving senselessly, loudly, unhappily from nowhere to nowhere. . . .[6]

Here, then, is the ultimate paradox: this faith which John senses is empty of meaning—repressive of his natural desires and less effective every day—serves a purpose even if it is one that is wholly negative. It saved the family from that growing, restless, directionless movement which is the curse of this age. Yet, in sparing them from "moving senselessly, loudly, unhappily from nowhere to nowhere. . .," it supplied them with nothing else. Despite John's growing awareness of the relative meaninglessness of the faith in which he was reared, he clings blindly to it. He meets Graut-baum, a young Communist, who tries to persuade him to join the party; but John will have none of it—not because of a firm conviction that Communism is evil but because of the hold his faith still exercises over him. When Graut-baum points out David's sexual adventures as an argument for the corruption of the church that he serves as a priest, John ends the argument and leaves him angrily.

When John witnesses by accident David's affair with Violet, however, he decides that he must forsake his religion; and this act of renunciation begins a new life for him and an allegiance to Communism. He realizes, nevertheless, that his allegiance to Communism is only a piece of not very clever self-deception. Before David's death, Violet calls the rectory; and when John answers the phone, Violet mistakes him for David and his reticence for the fact that his family is present in the room. When John suddenly realizes how much he resembles his brother, he is over-whelmed by the sense that he, too, is trapped, just as David and their grandfather were, in a life ruled by an emotion beyond their ability to control. Communism which now gives him license to indulge his sexual fantasies is no answer, for no rationalization offered by this new faith will help

him to understand his desires and the love which lurks behind them—not even David's death while in the midst of
his sins will help.

John's fears suggest a characteristic of Fielding's method
in this novel and in others he has written. The lack of resolution of John's problem occurs because Fielding understands John's plight as an artist, not as a philosopher. His
interest in John is not centered on drawing universally
applicable conclusions from the difficulties John faces;
instead, Fielding is interested in him as a human who
functions in a context incompatible with his ideals and his
hungers. That John's state is open to philosophical interpretation is without question; the difference, however, lies
in the fact that Fielding does not direct these universal
applications by infusing his own thoughts into those of his
protagonist. He does not conclude or solve; he intimates,
he suggests.

This intimation is possible because he restrains himself
from the great temptation which confronts most novelists:
the temptation to overdefine their characters—to produce
sharp, clear, absolute portraits. In John's character and in
those of the other personalities in the volume, the reader
discovers patches of vagueness which emanate from the
mystery which is at the core of humanity and the forces
which motivate it. Although no absolutely clear reason for
Mrs. Blaydon's action is given, the reader senses that her
actions flow from the very special relationships she has
established first with her father, then her husband, and
ultimately her children. Fielding makes no attempt to psy-
choanalyze her, nor does he try to manipulate the reader's
opinion of her. She is neither an ogre nor a caricature of a
doting, destructive mother. She is as human as are David
and John; and because of her humanity, no absolute position can be taken.

This lack of absolutes is the factor which draws the reader
into suspending disbelief that what he is witnessing is
true. John's world comes to resemble his own, for the territory John explores is as familiar to the reader as his own
life and as vaguely uncomfortable. This use of the familiar
is another characteristic of Fielding's method, one by means

of which he created his first literary work, "The Frog Prince."
Through a subtle alchemy, he redirected the fairy tale of
the enchanted prince and from it drew some fresh commentary which, though new, had all the comforts implicit
in the familiar.

In *Brotherly Love,* Fielding calls upon the long-established
tradition of the Anglican clergyman in English literature.
But unlike the treatment afforded by a Jane Austen or an
Anthony Trollope, the gentle ridicule to which the clergyman is generally subject is gone, as is his or anyone's placid,
enviable life ruffled only by the most minor of troubles.
In its place, Fielding projects the pain, unhappiness, and
turmoil generally associated with mankind's pilgrimage in
life. Important and apt, what better method could be used
to underscore the essential irony which is life? If the family
of a clergyman, supposedly closer to God than other individuals, can be inundated with difficulties, what can others
expect? Fielding may see no comfort in the familiar, the
accepted, the traditional since these elements represent
to him that thin layer of hypocrisy with which society covers
what it considers less than respectable in the vain hope
that concealment is equivalent to destruction.

But through this implied criticism there sometimes shines
that ideal life of spiritual strength and stability which is
the ultimate goal of John and his family. Unfortunately,
like most of mankind, they cannot perceive the road to this
goal even when they are presented with visible signs of it
in Father O'Brien. This life of stable spirituality lies not
in patterned formulas, which regulate prayer and the interrelationships of the members of the family, but comes through
the "sensed" rather than through the "known." John's
"fragile bowl" is the sight he is granted of this stratum of
human existence in which pure faith is capable of sustaining
life as it did his sister Mary's when no patterned formula,
no human agent, was successful. The reader senses, when
the volume ends, that John will have to discover this "sensed"
level of relationship and understanding with his fellow
man if his relationships and understanding are to be as
effective as Father O'Brien's prayers.

Again and again in the remaining volumes of the Blaydon

trilogy *(In the Time of Greenbloom* and *Through Streets Broad and Narrow)*, John is confronted with those difficulties which arise from a patterned, artificial relationship with those who enter his life. Only when he attains the level of the "sensed" does success, which is love, crown his efforts. Through this success comes a glimmer of hope, that hope he thought dead, as dead as his brother David. Moreover, other elements of the methods that Fielding uses in *Brotherly Love* appear in his remaining novels. Among these is the confusion between the ideal and reality which marks so many of John's decisions and the compromises he is forced to make which characterize his relationship to his brother. The unflawed idol, the object of John's childhood love, is tragically human; yet, ironically, it is no less an object for love. This conflict between what is and what John hopes things will be, Fielding limits only to the world of men. The woman, Mrs. Blaydon, has ideals, but they are eminently practical and attainable; and her presence and that of the other females in the volume serve to accentuate the conflict. They do so by sharing an equally disturbing desire, however; for where the males seek final, ideal resolutions to the eternal problems of life, the women seek to dominate those problems by preserving the status quo.

In Fielding's novels—and, indeed, in his poetry—man is the restless romantic; woman, the stabilizing, level-headed realist. Fielding does not argue with this point of view; he merely observes it to be so in the real world. Out of man's longings and woman's search for balance come, paradoxically, humanity's hope, its failures, and its achievements. Fielding's women tolerate, rather than forgive, the flaws that they detect in their men. Their role is that of Fielding's "safety valves": they dissipate pressures and prevent their men from destroying life which women understand as being essentially a long, never-ending series of compromises.

Like his understanding of women, Fielding's style in *Brotherly Love* is also found in his later work. His critics, almost unanimously, have not failed to cite the strengths of this aspect of his art. Almost all hold, like Dorothy Parker, that "it is a matter of grave doubt that Mr. Fielding could write anything, from a post card to a lexicon, without perception and pace and brilliance . . . so stunning a teller of tales and so inspired a creator of character." In terms of his characters, critics have noted his uncanny ability to develop three-dimensional characterizations for his minor as well as his major figures. In probing his method, they note that he achieves his effects by means of a scalpel-like precision in language that cuts through the superficialities with which human nature surrounds itself to reveal the character without developing a caricature or arriving at an absolute definition of the personality in question. Sometimes these characters are summarized in a phrase, more often by a gesture, or by a sudden reaction. All of his people, for that is what they become, are detailed, as Richard Hughes asserts, in "Brief, if blinding glimpses, thrown in as apparent asides."[7]

These "brief, if blinding glimpses" also characterize Fielding's technique of narrative. This technique—essentially a composite of irony, understatement, indirection, and suggestiveness in short, highly dramatic episodes—is so fashioned as not to intrude upon the consciousness of the reader. Events occur as if what is being narrated were reality. This nonintrusiveness extends also to those portions of the narrative wherein the sexual enters, for Fielding never descends to the clinical. But the point he makes in these episodes (notably in John's liaison with the Irish girl) is sharp, clear, and never lost. Fielding remains at all times plain and neutral, but the neutrality is not the product of indifference. The reader senses involvement—his own and the author's—in the events; and this sense of personal involvement grows from the suggestiveness that is an essential part of Fielding's style. This suggestiveness comes, in part, from understatement but more directly from the situations, characters, and themes which suggest parallels in the real world. Fielding uses the emotional pangs common to childhood and adolescence and all who are reaching for maturity and to those relationships which are part of that status.

Brotherly Love and the novels which follow it involve an individual who discovers that he is forced to devote himself, because of the circumstances surrounding the processes of maturation, more and more to appearances: to what seems rather than what really is. This play in which he finds himself the writer, producer, and star creates a tension and a sense of guilt which arise from a sensed need to resolve the dichotomy. This situation, in terms of John Blaydon, is examined in the remaining two volumes of the trilogy.

CHAPTER 3

In the Time of Greenbloom:
Love and Its Consequences

THE second chronological volume in the Blaydon
family trilogy and the second Fielding novel to be published, *In the Time of Greenbloom* was accorded unequiv-
ocal praise from the press. The English edition appeared
in August, 1956; by August of the following year, it received
its American publication, an event that introduced Fielding to his American public. By June, 1957, the book had
gone through its fourth printing in the United States, including a paperback edition. The English reviews, ranging
from the ecstatic to the profound, had convinced the American
publishers, William Morrow and Company, to add Fielding
to their growing list of authors. "Don't let's be short-sighted,"
an editorial department memo read (October 22, 1956),
"and let Scribner or Harcourt get Fielding." Acting under
this advice, negotiations proceeded apace; and, on November 13, 1956, a letter was dispatched welcoming Fielding
and noting that Adele Dogan was to be his editor.

The memo which urged that Fielding be given a contract
based on the success of *In the Time of Greenbloom* also
noted that the book would have great appeal for the "cogno-
scenti" rather than the "average reader." This same ob-
servation marks much of the English commentary, some of
which Morrow chose to quote on the dust jacket of the novel's
second printing. Evelyn Waugh, to whom Fielding had sent
a copy seeking his reaction, called it "a work of strong imagination and of dramatic invention." Frank Swinnerton praised
it as a book "for the connoisseur," and Margaret Willy noted
that it is "arresting . . . disturbing . . . written out of deep
understanding and wisdom." Others, like Kingsley Amis,
saw in the novel something of the method of its author's

forebear, Henry Fielding, in that it "combines the violent and the absurd, the grotesque and the romantic, the farcical and the horrific within a single novel."

American reviewers were no less enthusiastic. Paul Pickrel, writing in *Harper's*, called it "certainly one of the finest novels to come out of England since the second World War."[1] Orville Prescott praised it in *The New York Times* (June 2, 1957), likening Horab Greenbloom, one of the principal chracters, to the best of Evelyn Waugh's humorous creations. These comments, and the comfortable financial future they promised, gave impetus to Fielding's final decision to give up his medical practice in order to devote all of his energies to literature.

I *Analysis*

Shortly after Fielding's appointment as writer in residence at Washington State University in 1966, he delivered a lecture on the genesis of the novel, describing among other points his original plan for *In the Time of Greenbloom*. He wanted "to trace human love in all its directions, with all its vagaries, through the length of the book until the last sentence. I wanted to include childhood love, infantile love, incestuous love, parental love, sanctified love, unsanctified love, married love, widowed love, faithful love and the loves of infidelity through all their courses, and thus by the book's end map the misery, the contradictions and perhaps the glory of the loving animal."[2] In his own estimate, he fell far short of his goal. Nevertheless, despite his inability to achieve the emotional intensity of his goal, at one point or another he touches upon each aspect of love as he moves through the volume.

Like *Brotherly Love,* which precedes it in the trilogy, and *Through Streets Broad and Narrow,* which follows it, *In the Time of Greenbloom* is essentially a *Bildungsroman,* a "formation" novel or novel of education, one which focuses its attention on a central character and observes his youthful development. Often this type of novel is called an *Erziehungsroman* (*Erziehung,* "education" or "upbringing"; *roman,* novel) when it treats of the character's initiation and education in the hard realities of life. The form is ex-

tremely popular in the history of English literature, and
Henry Fielding's *Tom Jones* and Charles Dickens' *David
Copperfield* and *Oliver Twist* are classic examples.

Despite this thematic similarity of approach in Fielding's
three novels, *In the Time of Greenbloom* is closer to *Brotherly Love* than the other novel so far as the chronology of the
central figure, John Blaydon, is concerned. Both novels begin
in John's childhood and leave him as a young adult attending
medical school, but *Through Streets Broad and Narrow*
concentrates exclusively on the period covering his early
maturity. *In the Time of Greenbloom* differs radically from
its two companion volumes because it reflects, to a greater
degree, Fielding's growing understanding of humanity
and human relationships. Such an understanding, which
appeared embryonically in his first work, the poem "The
Frog Prince," deepened and broadened in *Brotherly Love*.
In terms of this developing understanding, *In the Time of
Greenbloom* represents a way-station in Fielding's career.
In a wider sense, however, the novel represents the opening
of new territory in his exploration of the human animal.
This new territory rests fundamentally on the sense of guilt
which permeates *Brotherly Love*, and is concerned with the
necessity for and the extent to which man's relationship
with man contributes to his stability in an unstable world.

Significantly, the novel opens with a description of Victoria, a young girl whom John and his sister, Melanie, meet
at a lawn party given by a neighbor, Mrs. Bellingham. Victoria, a strange little child, is only slightly older than John:
"The first thing he noticed about her was her whiteness:
she was a very white girl, as white in the face as the snow-
berries which grew under the elms at the foot of the vicarage
drive, and the skin of her delicate arms and legs was so pure
in its pallor that it was almost indistinguishable from the
tennis frock she was wearing" (1). She has an old-fashioned
quality about her, something that sets her apart from the
other children at the party, a quality that draws John to her.
In one sense, her clothing, the pallor of her skin, her very
name, suggest something from the past—an idea or an ideal
of purity and goodness that has no place in the present except to inspire. John senses, after a short conversation, that

they are very much alike; they are equally disdainful of the other children, equally searching for something they do not fully understand. After they agree to separate from the crowd and to meet later in the rose garden, John pins a rose to her dress, aping, in a manner, the conventional act he had observed the beau of his elder sister perform when he came to call on her.

This act draws them still closer emotionally. When Victoria suggests they go for a swim, John demurs, remarking that they have no bathing suits. Victoria, nevertheless, insists, laughing at his sense of shame. The pool they choose for their swim is interesting in and of itself; for, in many respects, it resembles the pool in E. M. Forster's *A Room With a View:* both pools are relatively shallow at their littorals but deeper in their centers; both are relatively small yet contain a frightening darkness in their depths. They are coincidentally similar, perhaps, except for the fact that both authors use them for a similar purpose: in Forster's novel, George Emerson, much like John Blaydon, is persuaded to swim in the pond; and, like John, he is reluctant to undress. When he does and plunges into the water, he begins to sense remotely the true meaning Lucy has for him; and John, through his swim, senses the depths of his attachment for Victoria. Like George, John realizes that, in some mysterious way, this girl is part of him; he, part of her.

Shortly after John and Victoria plunge into the water, he hears her cries for help. Frantically, he swims out to her only to discover that she has disappeared into the dark depths of the pond. Heedless of the dangers of those depths, he dives after her, frantically searches for her, and finally discovers her white form in the darkness. As he swims with her limp body to the landing, Melanie and Tim, another guest, appear at the water's edge; for they had been searching for the two for some time. Melanie shouts in derision about their nudity to an unmindful John who is filled with only one thought, the salvation of Victoria, whom he fully realizes, with a pang, that he loves and whom he believes is dead. With Tim's help, he carries her white body to higher ground and gives her artificial respiration. Suddenly, while he is astride the reviving girl, Mrs. Bellingham breaks into the clearing—like the representative of the mature world the two children had hoped to escape. Her look of horror tells John that she thinks the worst of what she sees, and he is shocked by her questions and realizes that no assurances from him will convince her of his innocence. Mrs. Bellingham is beyond the point, however, of caring about the morality of the scene; her only thought is to hide from others what she is convinced has occurred between the two children.

Later, when John and Melanie return home, Melanie hastens to tell Mrs. Blaydon of all that has occurred, as John knew she would. (This is the first appearance of Mrs. Blaydon in the volume, and the role Fielding gives her to play is significant.) Like some avenging angel, Mrs. Blaydon pulls John out to the summer house to question him. Although she is also the concerned mother fearful of what the incident will do to her child, John sees her only as the pursuer of guilt. She questions him sharply; and when she is finally convinced that nothing sexual occurred, she nevertheless pursues the point. "Did you look at her?" He doesn't answer. The question comes more pointedly. "Yes," he says, "Yes I did—in a way." She draws breath to reply, but before she can utter the words, he explodes. "But *that* wasn't wrong, not to *see*. I didn't *look*, I *saw!* If other people want to turn seeing into looking, it's they who are wrong, not me, isn't it?" The very vehemence of his reply suggests the weakness of his belief in what he has said. Mrs. Blaydon answers, "No! But—" and never finishes. She hurries out of the summer house. John turns to look in the cracked mirror in the dimming light and discovers a figure tall and thin and pale as Victoria. The shadows cling "like a fine dark hair to the temples of his forehead" (37–38).

John's education proceeds apace in Chapter II, "The First Wedding," in which he discovers several other facets of his character and of the people with whom he is involved. He does not clearly understand, as yet, the implications of what he has lived through in the first chapter: the essential hypocrisy of the mature, the meaning Victoria has for him, and the growing sense of guilt permeating his relationship with her that has been initiated by Mrs. Bellingham's reaction and underscored by his mother's questioning. He is relatively untouched by these matters because he is still a child living for coming events which hold the promise of joy. He is desperate to attend the wedding of his favorite brother, David; and, when an indiscretion he committed in his French class causes his confinement to school, he is heartbroken. In the dormitory, after the lights have been put out, he is approached by Marston, with whom he has been friendly and who, in some way, reminds him of Victoria. This similarity forces him to realize that

he wanted to be loved as much as he wanted to love. Who was Victoria and who was he? This he realized suddenly was what he wanted all the time; this which was happening now was the measure of his greed for her and its only true expression and the wedding, and the marriage of their two selves, of the self that wanted to be loved and the self that wanted only to love must end like this. In some mysterious way the self that was Victoria could only finally unite into a self that was them both, in a darkness, a secrecy, and a delight that was like this. (57)

Suddenly, Marston's true intent breaks through John's reverie, John repels him loudly, they fight, and John draws blood. The incident leads to the "Badger," the headmaster; and the boys are forced to settle the matter in a fight presided over by another master "Toad." John loses the battle, but his punishment, nevertheless, is deferred even though the implication is that he had initiated the incident. Once again, John's true intentions are misunderstood by the adult world; but this problem is put aside when he learns that he will be permitted to attend the wedding. His heart beats in antici- pation: Victoria will be there when David weds his Prudence Cable.

The wedding and the reception that follows it are strained. During the ceremony, John tries desperately to think only of Victoria and not the gathering clouds presaging a coming conflict between the mothers-in-law. He prays that nothing will go wrong, that his mother will say nothing; finally, in desperation, he offers prayers to the effect that he will not think of Victoria if God will let peace reign.

The reception is tense with the impending battle between Mrs. Cable, Prudence's mother, and Mrs. Blaydon, both of

whom arm themselves out of love for their children. Mrs.
Cable enjoys her social position and is careful that all
note how well placed she is, and Mrs. Blaydon, sensitive
to the slight she sees offered to her son in Mrs. Cable's
posture and even more sensitive of the country accents of the
guests she has invited from Yorkshire, rankles when Mrs.
Cable's darts penetrate. John, distracted by the presence of
Victoria, is at first unaware that the battle has begun. Finally,
when the storm bursts in full force, he is confused by the
sharp remarks; but then he

thought of the boxing match with Marston and realized with dis-
may that what he had witnessed had been only a repetition of it
in the world of the grownups. Mother and Mrs. Cable had fought
in public just as he and Marston had fought in private, and there
had been no older proportionate Toad to oversee the fight. They
had mauled and hurt each other over their love for David and
Prudence with no one to see fair play or establish a reason for
their fight. The comparison had sickened him; he did not want
to feel sorry for anyone; . . . he wanted to be . . . changing sides if
necessary, sure of his sympathies and ready to champion Mother
or Mrs. Cable to the death but he could not. (95)

John is confused, as only a child can be confused, by a vision
of the adult world without its mask. He expected different
behavior from adults because of the certitude they exude in
their relationships with each other. Ironically, his grasp
of the cause of the parents' situation is surer and firmer than
that of any adult present. Only his thoughts of Victoria save
him from complete disappointment in the wedding, for he
will see her shortly at holidaytime in Danbey Dale.

Chapter III, "In Danbey Dale," describes John's deepening attachment for Victoria and the widening scope of her
meaning for him. The title, ironically, suggests a nursery
rhyme; indeed, Fielding opens the chapter by quoting the
first two stanzas of his poem "Bo Peep" in which the poet
admonishes the shepherdess for calling back her sheep
who have wandered off. Like the sheep of the poem, Victoria and John have wandered into "pale pastures leading
up to mountains." The watchful eye of reality, maturity,
has awakened, however, to call them to "some white water-

shed of earth and sky." The chapter opens with John musing on the consequences of his family's departure from the vicarage at Beddington for Anglesey, for the move suggests the end of his childhood and a change in the relationship he has established with Victoria. His thoughts cause him to be late for his appointment with the girl, who guesses correctly the reason for his lateness for their picnic in a nearby cave. When John meets her and they are on their way back to the farm where her mother is staying, Victoria taunts John good-naturedly about his love for her by telling him about a blond hiker whom she has met earlier in the day. She relates how she sensed that he had wanted to kiss her. John, disturbed by her banter, tries desperately and awkwardly to tell her how much he loves her.

When they arrive at the home where she and Mrs. Blount, her mother, are staying as guests of George Harkness, her mother's lover, the children find the adults impatient for lunch. Harkness, though large and masculine, seems unsure of himself; but he wants to marry Mrs. Blount, whose husband, Victoria's father, has divorced her. During the meal, Harkness and Mrs. Blount are subtly and ironically juxtaposed to John and Victoria in their emotional relationships to each other. Harkness is insensitive, almost boorish; Mrs. Blount is a caricature of her daughter. After lunch, the children start for the cave and their picnic; but the joy of the outing is clouded for John by Victoria's taunting and by her growing presentiment of doom. "Nothing could happen to me when I'm with you, could it?" she says. The question frightens John, who senses from it and from an earlier equally frightening conversation about death that in some way he will be losing her, but he hastens to reassure and comfort her and himself.

In the cave, they set about preparing tea. When Victoria grows increasingly more nervous, John does his best to calm her. They have settled down to their picnic when, suddenly, they hear someone whistling a strange tune. Frightened, they call out. "Not very far away, in the tunnel, perhaps, perhaps behind him in some other part of the gallery, somebody swore pleasurably, an obscene, lingered-over word." When the owner of the voice appears, he is the hiker Victoria had met earlier that morning. To John's disgust the intruder plays court to Victoria; and, beneath the smoothness of his words, John senses danger. Nothing John does or says seems to move the stranger to understand that he is not wanted. John grows increasingly uneasy under the "oiliness" of the hiker's words; Victoria becomes more relaxed. She chides John for his fright. They conclude their tea and leave the cave none too soon for John, whose apprehensiveness grows.

Through deft questioning and flattery, the stranger discovers that Victoria's parents are divorced and that she and her mother are visiting at the Harkness farm. John tries once again in desperation to get rid of him, but to no avail. The hiker follows the children home; and when Victoria finds a letter of her mother's in the pocket of her Mackintosh that she had promised to post, the stranger offers to drive her to the post office. Although John objects vehemently, Victoria leaves with him. John has nothing to do but wait, a wait which brings a darkening of the cloud of apprehension which has hovered over the afternoon. Did Victoria really care for him? Girls, as his brothers were continually drumming into him, always were attracted to men older than themselves.

He wanders into the farmyard to the barn and releases Harkness's dogs. Entering the house, with the dogs trailing after, suspicious of his movements, he hears the noise of a bedspring in the upstairs bedroom. Bounding up the stairs and shouting a warning, he throws open the door and discovers Mrs. Blount and George Harkness in bed. Later, when it is evident that Victoria has disappeared, Harkness, after questioning John as to her whereabouts, forces him to lie about discovering him and Victoria's mother together. The scene disgusts John because it is somewhat reminiscent of what had occurred to him when Mrs. Bellingham had found him astride Victoria. When the questioning about Victoria begins in earnest, the police suspect that John had a hand in Victoria's disappearance. After a long search which leads back to the interior of the cave and the site of the ill-fated picnic, they discover Victoria's body very close to the scene of the picnic. Victoria's death crushes John.

Chapter IV, "In the Time of Greenbloom," treats of John's

deepening depression and his growing sense of guilt against which he is powerless. Like the preceding chapter and all of others in the volume, this chapter begins with a quotation from one of Fielding's poems, in this instance the first four lines of the fourth stanza of "Soliloquy at Evening over the Channel": "No Angel knows/No fire-hung Seraph knows or could/What I, the fallen son of fallen fathers/Now and then within the cirrus understood." John, like the persona in the poem, possesses knowledge which no one else has: his memory of the presence of Victoria in his life and what she meant to him. He cannot forget her nor fill the void left by her death, nor can he avoid the publicity that surrounded him after the discovery of her body. Because of this publicity, he is asked to leave Beowulf's, the public school to which he was sent after her death. He is indifferent to his fate as he becomes locked within a growing and incomprehensible sense of guilt.

One day, Michael, his brother, takes him for an outing which ends in Balliol College in the rooms of Horab Greenbloom. Greenbloom is a rich eccentric, intellectually exciting and emotionally perceptive, who is wildly intrigued by the bizarre; and he, himself, is bizarre with his wooden leg and in his living habits. In his selfishness, he is completely the child, but otherwise totally adult. Significantly, his intellectual life centers upon a book he is producing which is as agonizingly difficult as its subject, the philosophy of Ludwig Wittgenstein; for his goal is to clarify what is obscure in Wittgenstein's philosophy. He has already begun his task; but, characteristic of his approach to all things, he has begun the work with its last chapter and is proceeding slowly to the first.

John is completely overwhelmed by Greenbloom's presence, for he has never met anyone quite like him. In the tragedy which has engulfed him, all the adults John has hitherto known have been totally ineffectual in their attempts to help him. Only Greenbloom is able to penetrate his tragic sense of guilt to present to him another dimension: the life of the mind. When Greenbloom wildly suggests a flight to France in his airplane, Michael demurs, but finally relents. A short detour to pick up Greenbloom's beautiful fiancée, Rachel, precedes the compulsive flight. A miscalculation takes them to Ireland with hilarious results.

In "Rooker's Close," section 5, John attends the tutoring school suggested by Mr. Rudmose, the master of Beowulf's. He takes an assumed name, Joseph Bowden, to conceal his identity; relaxes somewhat in his new-found anonymity, and quickly falls in step with the life of the school. Mr. Victor, a convert from Judaism, is headmaster; and he sees his new faith, Anglicanism, as the means whereby he can identify himself as English. He rules the school with an iron hand, and John thinks of him as a "snake" who expected his "rabbits," his students, to remain still under his guidance. Like Victor, the boys in his care have very little real use for religion, except for a day student who is Catholic and is the butt of the boys' jokes. Despite Mr. Victor's essential indifference to religion, John adheres strictly to the formulas of the faith he has adopted. When Victor tries to question John about Victoria's death, he makes him promise, despite John's protests, to go to confession. Mr. Victor's insistence proceeds from his concern about the publicity which might come from the news of John's true identity and his certitude that his school and himself hold the answer to John's problem.

Before the time set for John's confession, he decides to go to the local beach for a swim. There he comes upon two attractive girls whom he has seen before and who have aroused his interest. He longs for the "sureness of purpose and ease of manner" used by the young men who flock about them. One day, he hopes, he will be as relaxed as they: "But secretly he knew that this would never be so, that all his life he would have to guess at behavior, walk carefully and watch as narrowly as a tramp at table." Suddenly, when his reverie is broken by a whistled tune so strange yet so familiar, he is certain that he has heard the same tune in the cave before the stranger had appeared. He wildly searches about until his eyes light on one of the admirers of the two girls he had been studying so intently; and he tries desperately to accuse the man of the crime. When he realizes that he cannot penetrate his defenses, John accuses the stranger of stealing his wallet while he was attempting to get the man to the police. His accusations produce a furor and an effect opposite to that which he had intended. Frustrated, he drops the charges when one of the students from his school recognizes him in the midst of the curious crowd that had gathered. John, confused by the appearance of the boy and by the possible loss of his comfortable anonymity, realizes that his scheme will not work. In his haste to get away, he brushes aside the incident with the reminder that they are due back at school by five.

Before returning to the school, John stops at St. Jude's for the confession he has promised to make. He cannot concentrate on the preparation before he confesses, so indifferent is he to the merits of what he is about to do. He knows that he will have to present a convincing catalog of his faults if he is not to be considered "snide." The confession begins unpromisingly; but Father Delura, reserved and cool, encourages him. Suddenly, John tells him of Victoria and her death. In a passion he tells the priest "I want to be forgiven for something I never did as well as for the things I did do. . . ." Father Delura, disturbed by what he hears, admonishes John: "I think you had better say no more at present. I am not sure that you are well." Before dismissing him, he asks John if there is anything else he would like to say; and John replies, "Can you tell me why I feel that I ought to be forgiven for something I never did? Why do I keep thinking about it all the time? Why have I felt different ever since it happened? Was it wrong of me to love her? Is that why I go on and on like this? Will I never be the same again? Happy like other people?"

Father Delura has no answer to John's questions. Frustrated, the young man returns to a pew on which is affixed a sign: "This Pew Was Occupied by H. M. King Edward VII On the Occasion of His Visit to Worthing September 1905." That and the bloodless crucifix on the rood screen are the last objects he sees as he leaves the church forever. Like the John of *Brotherly Love*, he has discovered that his Anglican faith, willed to him by the generation which affixed the commemorative plaque on the pew, is empty and meaningless, incapable of supplying comfort and help when needed.

Crestfallen, John returns to the school only to be accosted

by Mr. Victor who accuses him, after he blunders over his explanation of what occurred at the beach, of seeking illicit sexual adventures with the girls on the beach. John, who can take no more, explodes. Finally, after his anger burns itself out, he sips the tea offered him and "wondered what did it all matter. . . . Nothing was important because nothing was true." Mr. Victor, ruffled, closes the interview with a suggestion that he ought to leave Rooker's Close. In the final chapter, "Island Summer," John has joined his family on Anglesey, the scene of several events in *Brotherly Love*. His despondency has grown even deeper: his longing for Victoria has been sharpened by his heightened sense of guilt over her death; and a new element has been added, his growing fear for the future. He has failed at school, failed to find an emotionally satisfying friendship, failed to find love. His mind dwells on suicide—a long swim away from shore and peace for his troubled soul.

In the midst of his depression, his brother brings Greenbloom to visit the family. Mrs. Blaydon is a bit distressed by the visit, but she nevertheless attempts to ask him to donate a sum for the new rood screen. That visit, and the long introspective talk which passes between him and Greenbloom, turns John from his wish for death. Eventually, he meets Dymphna, aptly named after the patron saint of the emotionally ill. An Irish girl, who reminds him of Victoria, she helps him to new insights into his sorrows and frustrations. As the novel ends, she leads John to the threshold of an understanding of himself.

II *Comparison of* Brotherly Love
and In The Time of Greenbloom

Structurally, *In the Time of Greenbloom* does not differ radically from *Brotherly Love*. Fielding develops the novel through a similar use of clusters of dramatic episodes that are charged with a series of ironic and paradoxical contrasts of character, incident, and tone. The purity and innocence of John's love for Victoria is sharply contrasted with the emotional attachment of Harkness for Mrs. Blount; the hypocrisy of the adult world is vividly juxtaposed to the

elemental honesty of youth. Fielding's use of color underscores the irony implicit in these relationships; from the
very beginning, he associates the color white with Victoria. Her color, the first element that attracts John to her,
suggests the nature of the young who approach life in terms
of absolutes, blacks and whites, rather than the greys, the
compromises of the adult world.

The similarity in structural development of the two novels
continues in the manner in which Fielding groups the six
chapters in *In the Time of Greenbloom*. Each chapter is
almost as independent as a short story, as are those in *Brotherly Love;* but they break naturally into two distinct but vitally
related parts. The first three chapters treat of John's early
adolescence and his discovery of his attachment for Victoria; the second group explores his later adolescence and
the effects of Victoria's violent death upon his maturing
emotional life. A pivotal situation turns the plot and atmosphere in the novel, just as one is included in *Brotherly
Love;* but there is a difference. In *Brotherly Love,* Fielding
devotes an entire chapter to David's seduction of John's girl
friend; in *In the Time of Greenbloom,* a single ironic and
subtly understated moment within the third chapter serves
as the pivot: John's realization that Victoria is dead.

Structural similarity between the two novels does not end
here. Like *Brotherly Love, In the Time of Greenbloom*
probes the tragic, yet comic implications of life; but the
probing differs, in indirection and elusiveness. *Brotherly
Love* comes close to allegory, but *In the Time of Greenbloom*
always remains in the realm of metaphor. Allegory is too
pat an approach for Fielding, who senses, to a greater degree
in this volume, that absolute reasons and conclusions con-
cerning human relationships are rarely achievable in life.
Hence, a greater degree of mystery and indirection occurs
in his approach to character. Fewer answers are given; fewer
absolutes created.

Another difference in Fielding's approach to the implications of tragedy and comedy in life is the expansion through
another dimension. Dr. Frank Towne, chairman of the Department of English at Washington State University, discusses this dimension in an unpublished article:

This particular technique by which Mr. Fielding contrives to make the tragic bear upon the comic and the comic upon the tragic is to cause a number of comic and tragic potentialities and memories to converge in a single incident in such a way that they fuse for a moment and then go their separate ways. It is as though rays of light of various colors were brought together by a prism for a short space and then dispersed by another prism—except that when the comic and tragic elements converge and produce a tragicomic unit, we are still able to distinguish the individual elements of which the unity is composed. There is a mystery in perception of this kind, reminiscent of Dante's glimpse of the Holy Trinity as three circles of light of different colors all occupying the same space.

This technique which Dr. Towne describes arises essentially from the anecdotal quality of Fielding's work. He supplies his readers with a wealth of incident and comic characters from which proceeds a subject matter filled with comic potentialities and overtones which are, as Dr. Towne observes, something more than comic. Fielding offers insights, through this subject matter, into the vicissitudes of the interior life and the natural history of human emotions which are fundamentally tragic. Many incidents reveal the depths of his technique, but the most significant ones are the two that Fielding ironically juxtaposes: the first involves the events at the pool; the second, the discovery of Mrs. Blount and Harkness by John.

The scene at the pool in the first chapter has all the trappings of serious romance and is somewhat reminiscent of a ballet. Indeed, the reader is persuaded to recall the romantic setting of a ballet by the chapter's title, "L'Après-Midi," and by the short poem with which Fielding chooses to begin it. The poem, which speaks of "the spectre is the rose," recalls the romantic ballet of the same name. The properties in the scene are as seriously romantic as the ballets they suggest: the heavily wooded glade, the dark pool on which gracefully float elegant white swans, the stillness, and most of all, the two lovers who have stolen away from the world to reveal their love for each other. Comedy enters, however, when the reader realizes that the lovers are not beautiful, graceful creatures like the swans but gangling preadolescents

with gawky bodies. Their love tryst is not capped by a series
of passionate embraces but by a swim in the pool.

The smile which the realities of the scene bring to the
lips is quickly replaced by the tragedy of Victoria's cries
for help and by John's frantic efforts to save her from drowning. This tragedy is swiftly followed by Mrs. Bellingham's
reaction when she sees the nude John astride an equally nude
Victoria, and this scene brings to the mind of the reader the
almost classical humorous situation of burlesque in which
the irate, cuckolded husband discovers his wife and her
lover. The humorous scene is followed by tragic implications:
Mrs. Bellingham truly believes that something evil has
occurred; but even more tragic, this belief does not disturb
her as much as her desire to gloss over the incident to prevent others from knowing that it had occurred in her garden.
The real tragedy is her indifference to the human element
and, by implication, the indifference of the world and society which she represents.

Like this scene, John's discovery of Mrs. Blount and her
lover is fraught with comic as well as tragic implications. In
this instance, he assumes the role Mrs. Bellingham played
earlier in the book; unlike her, however, he represents youth
and its idealism coming into conflict with maturity and its
penchant for dissimilation. Mrs. Blount and George Harkness
have seized the opportunity afforded by the absence of the
children to enjoy their love affair; but ironically, Victoria
and John's has also proceeded apace. The humor of John's
discovery is tinged into tragedy by the sordidness of the
conduct of the adults, but Harkness's haste to force John
to alter the facts of the discovery are also humorous. But
the comic implications of the scene congeal into the depths
of tragedy when the reader senses by implication that John's
discovery must have coincided with Victoria's rape and
murder. The scene becomes a gross parody of her pain.

To understand more fundamentally the ironic and paradoxical presence in Fielding's work of the tragic in the comic
and the comic in the tragic, the thought of the Christian
Existentialist philosopher, Gabriel Marcel, is relevant because Fielding is much drawn to his work. At the core of
Marcel's philosophy is a sharp, unwavering conviction of

the absolute absurdity of life. Man can achieve high stations, vast wealth, luxuriate in the joys of the palate, mind, body, emotions, but all is subject to termination by that "incurable disease" to which all succumb. To understand man's plight in this narrow, materialistic sense, is to taste the tragedy that is life. Such an understanding can lead logically only to suicide, for why should man endure the pain and the absence of these delights when he can end life at its apogee of delight?

Man has a life, however, other than that of material joy and of material extension: he has open to him the life of love. To live the life of love, which is the gift of God, is to apprehend the materially oriented life in the full light of its absurdity and comic implications. To live the life of love is, in a sense, to rob life of its tragedy. No loss of material pleasure can affect one's stability nor destroy one's hope because love is essentially the key to a balanced view of life. John Blaydon senses the truth of this position. Because he has lost love, he has lost his ability to measure life. But he has lost more. Love is the key to all because it unlocks the mysteries that go beyond the limitations of the human intellect and of nature itself. Love gives a sensed knowledge of others, that type of knowledge John gained about Victoria before she died. Through this emotional knowledge of others comes knowledge of self, and to know oneself is to exist. In other words, love generates existence.

John, in losing Victoria, has lost himself. Only through her, in whom he sees himself so often, can he perceive the world. Otherwise, the world as Marcel puts it, is like a "broken watch" which to the eye appears sound but "put the watch to your ear and you don't hear any ticking."[3] To John, love is more than a means for understanding and a signpost or guide through a broken world. Love becomes the guide to the final end of things: he desires to be forgiven, and he hopes in that way to reach God in whom he believes. Love leads to the conviction, held by Juliana of Norwich, the medieval Christian mystic whom Fielding admires, that "all will be well, and all manner of things will be well."

In the light of Gabriel Marcel's position and from Fielding's posture in the novel, no impenetrable mystery surrounds the sense of guilt which seems to overwhelm John. True, some measure of guilt can be ascribed to the frustrated sexual desires latent in John's position and to that degree of guilt surrounding his brother and grandfather in *Brotherly Love*. But the larger measure of his guilt comes to him because he senses the death of his very being in the death of Victoria, the object of his love. In reaching out to her through love, he was in the process of giving life to himself; with her death, he died like an aborted foetus. He is physically alive but existentially dead. This death—his guilt—disturbs him. He is constantly mocked by the life he witnesses in others; but his condition is essentially ironic, for those he believes alive are themselves dead because they center their lives not in love of others but in themselves. What John is not aware of is the fact that they are consummate actors: Mrs. Blount, Mrs. Bellingham, Victor, Harness and even Rudmose, who finally commits suicide—the act which to Gabriel Marcel is the only answer to the material life.

When Greenbloom, like a savior, comes, he insists on involvement, the prelude to love, and ultimately, to existence. Only by sensing Greenbloom's genuine interest in him does John sense the beginning of the end of his nonexistence. Greenbloom breaks down all barriers, overpowers all defenses, conquers all indifference by his exuberance. At the core of his being burns the principle that Fielding admires so in the philosophy of Martin Buber; and to the degree to which the principle motivates Greenbloom, he fittingly personifies that principle. Buber uses the word *Begegnung*, "meeting" or "relationship," to summarize what is often called the "I-Thou" theory after his volume *I and Thou*. The relationship is essentially a principle of engagement of individual with thing and of the individual with individual. Through that engagement flows the Eternal Thou, God, life, love, or whatever one wishes to call that "wholly other."

This lesson of involvement which Greenbloom has learned so well, this necessity to bring "God into the world," underscores and intensifies John's guilt. Like Dostoevski's characters who tear themselves apart in agonizing self-examination, probings of inner motivations, and monumental restlessness, John needs and longs for the presence of

God whom he has the power to bring into the world by communion with others. He soon discovers that the formulas
of the faith of his childhood are not the answer to seemingly
unassuageable desire. A Jew, ironically, yet significantly,
brings him, a Christian, to the threshold of existence and
to God through his persistence, somewhat in the manner
in which Leopold Bloom influences Stephen in Joyce's
Ulysses. Without Greenbloom, there could be no Dymphna
and no beginning to the end of John's guilt.

In the light of Fielding's clarification of the essence of
John's *Angst, In the Time of Greenbloom* builds upon the
relationships limned in *Brotherly Love*. In that novel, John's
problems are understood only dimly and tangentially in
terms of the interrelationships of the Blaydon family and
notably through his emotional attachment for his brother,
David. In *In the Time of Greenbloom*, John's difficulties
are viewed on the larger canvas of an individual who is
maturing in a world that is essentially dead. For all its strife,
its pain, its turmoil, the Blaydon family in *Brotherly Love*
is alive because its members love one another. Like all of
humanity, John must, in the normal course of events, leave
the "I-Thou" existence of family life and move to another
level of existence, one that is established through the love
of man and woman. Like so many individuals who move
toward such love, his efforts are thwarted. In his case, a
horrible calamity wrought by an unknown stranger—an
incomprehensible and unidentifiable evil—blocks his path.
Unless he establishes another pattern of interrelationships
similar to the one he lost with Victoria's death, he will remain
existentially dead.

In the light of John's predicament, therefore, the two
volumes suggest a metaphor for the central problem of life
as Fielding understands it and as he develops it from the
philosophies of Gabriel Marcel and Martin Buber. Simply
stated, Fielding implies that man must struggle for existence
through emotional engagement with others. Through that
existence comes the balance and the understanding of the
totality of creation that is needed in a world essentially dead
because of its involvement only in things. He also suggests
that true existence is not the result of a single act or of a
single instance of engagement and involvement; instead,

existence is an ever-recurring experience on as many levels as there are individuals encountered. To narrow engagement with one's fellow man is to narrow existence, and to narrow existence is to limit God's entry into the world and to that communion He desires with His creatures.

Aside from broadening his canvas and clarifying the philosophical core of *Brotherly Love, In the Time of Green-bloom* reiterates Fielding's posture toward his characters. Again, as in his very first work, he creates his women as essentially more stable than his men. They seek a balance, an order, a stability, and a surface calm even when not motivated by the best of intentions, as is evidenced by Mrs. Bellingham's and Mrs. Blount's actions. Mrs. Blount, though as passionately involved with Harkness as he is with her, manages to retain her composure when he loses his. Fielding's men, on the other hand, are pure romantics who are emotionally alive to the ideals toward which they strive; and they are restless, unsure of themselves, questioning, always eager, rarely satisfied.

Fielding also continues to draw upon his personal experiences and friendships for models for his characters. Many of John's experiences are taken from Fielding's own life. Members of his family appear in the pages of the book: Mr. and Mrs. Barnsley, as the senior Blaydons: his sister, Mary, as Melanie; and his brother, Michael, as himself. During the course of a talk on the genesis of the novel, Fielding identified yet another individual, who became Greenbloom, from his own experience whom he used in the novel. Fielding, when speaking of him, gives him the fictional name he created:

. . . one night a large Bentley rolled up the drive and three people got out of it, my brother Michael, his friend Greenbloom and Greenbloom's delicious fiancée, Rachel. The two men had driven from Oxford and picked up Rachel and her diamonds on the way. Greenbloom brought with him his limp, his damaged leg—his special knife and fork and plate which when my father inadvertently used them had to be buried for twenty-four hours in the garden before he himself might touch them again. My uncle Daggo too had a predilection for getting hold of these things—and Greenbloom always knew. It was rather like "Who's been sleeping in my bed?" But more than all that—into a Christian house, muddled, quarrelsome, full of love and the best and worst intentions, Green-bloom brought his Jewishness, his riches and from my point of view, best of all, his fiancee.

Like the fictional Greenbloom, the real one brought a breath of fresh air into young Fielding's life; for no one or nothing he had encountered had had quite the same effect on him. Fielding had been suffering from an unrequited adolescent love affair with a "bronzed tennis-playing girl called Esme," and Greenbloom's exoticism and more especially Rachel, who also finds a place in his novel, did much to ease John's pain.

Victoria, too, comes from Fielding's past, for she is based, in part, on his dimly remembered first love. "I knew that she was not quite real, that she was an idea more than a person, that like love itself she was in my mind more than she was in herself, in her own clothes, which nevertheless I took such trouble to describe." The clothes he speaks of are those the character wears when the reader first meets her. She is completely in white, suitable, of course for playing tennis which she is doing, but suggestive of the unreality of her existence. Her very name, Victoria, implies some element dimly remembered from the past which, in fading, grows dearer. She is the ideal, unconsummated love formerly possessed, which clearly he can never more possess.

Once, in a conversation (August 15, 1967, at Pullman, Washington), Fielding enlarged upon the genesis of the character of Victoria. He recalled a young lady in one of his father's parishes, Margaret Maule, by name, who was suffering from an advanced state of tuberculosis. The disease had given her a skin of almost translucent whiteness that made her appear delicately ethereal. Like Victoria at the opening of the volume, she impressed Fielding as someone whose whole being was focused on another world. He recalled yet another young lady in a different parish of his father's, Marjorie Bellwood, whose fate contributed to the closing moments of Victoria's life. Fielding remembers her as a beautiful girl who was involved in a horrible accident which resulted in her death. He recalls the sight of her white, limp body covered with blood in the arms of her would-be rescuer. The sight was too painful for him to describe; therefore, the limp, broken body appears only by implication in the novel. The sight of Victoria's ravished body is the more painful to the reader because of Fielding's sensitivity.

Fielding confesses, however, that Victoria is more than a composite of a dimly remembered childhood love affair and of two singular acquaintances. She owes her life in part to the influence of Emily Brontë's *Wuthering Heights*, for she is as much Kathy of that volume as she is anyone. Like Kathy's, Victoria's attraction for John, who in the same sense resembles Heathcliff, rests on an emotional attachment which is intellectually indecipherable. Victoria is as wild, as positive, as unattainable as Kathy. Her very being, too, grows in proportion to her attachment to her lover. When the two are separated, dire consequences follow. John is as lost as Heathcliff.

The character, John Blaydon, however, does not approach that of Heathcliff as that of Victoria approaches that of Kathy. There are elements of Fielding in John, but also there exists a quality in John which bursts the boundaries of autobiography. This quality—his suffering—universalizes his character. When Fielding was asked about the significance of his use of the name "John," his first reaction was that it is a common name among the English. Other implications were discussed, however, including the biblical significance of the name. John's initials, J.B., are those used for the title of a verse play by Archibald MacLeish based on the Job legend; and John's suffering, like Job's, is not of his own making. Again, the initials suggest John the Baptist; and John Blaydon, too, is a "voice of one crying in the wilderness." Like that prophet, he shares the same loneliness common to all who are dissatisfied and seek for a fulfillment of themselves and their potentialities in a world hostile to such fulfillment. Much of John's character in this restless biblical sense is also evident in Dr. Chance, the central figure of *Eight Days*, Fielding's third novel and his first departure from the Blaydon cycle.

CHAPTER 4

A Journey Through Hell and a Return to the Blaydon Family

I Eight Days: *Genesis and Critical Reaction*

ON October 4, 1956, the editorial offices of William Morrow and Company received a letter from Gabriel Fielding containing a description of the genesis of a new novel which was to represent a radical departure from the subject matter but not the theme of the Blaydon trilogy, two volumes of which had already been published. "My new novel," he wrote, "to be called *Eight Days*, is set in the International Zone of Tangier and is the outcome of a brief holiday I spent there in October of last year." Fielding had intended to use the leisurely vacation to plan the structure of the third volume of the Blaydon trilogy, but he never progressed very far: "Within two days of my arrival, I had to pack away my manuscript and my pen and forget all about my trilogy for the time being." He became involved in a series of incidents which were "nearly fantastic and very frightening," and "there was a time when I thought I would never leave Tangier alive." These "nearly fantastic incidents" later became the source of the plot of his third novel.

He spent those memorable eight days of his holiday in a "strange sort of imprisonment" in a large, well-lighted penthouse in the American sector of the International Zone. In addition to himself, the penthouse was occupied by a dying American millionaire and his very beautiful, much younger bride who were on their honeymoon. Fielding was called to the apartment in his professional capacity as a doctor to minister to the man; as it chanced, the man was a Roman Catholic, and Fielding had become a convert only a short time before. The man, it turned out, was in need

of more than medical attention; for he was a victim of black-
mail, like Macgrady in *Eight Days*. Five men were his
enemies: "They were not young; they were in fact the most
dangerous sort of criminal: well bred, educated, monied,
perverted and old enough to have no fear of death either
for themselves or for anyone else." These are the characteristics Fielding gives their counterparts in the book
he later shaped from his experiences.

Another element of that strange holiday, however, helped
to develop the novel:

Behind us all was the northern part of the African continent,
around us was the population of the International Zone: Arabs,
Seraphino, Spaniards, Gibraltese, French, Italians, exiled Ameri-
cans and crypto-Russians. We were on the thick edge of the Sahara
desert and on the edge, too, of the pan-Arabianism which President
Nasser is at present staking his claim to dictatorship. We knew
what was happening in the political sense long before the advent of
the Suez crisis; we knew a great deal more, because we heard
everything and in one sense could see almost as far ahead as 1958;
but we were not particularly interested. The first murmurs of a
desert war between Russia and America did not matter very much
to us against the immediacy of our own urgent concerns; I mean our
Catholicism, and the imminent death of one of us.

Fielding added other personal experiences to those encountered on his strange holiday, notably those he had as a
prison doctor. While working in that capacity, he came
across a strange individual who served as the source of
Marcovicz's warped character. The man, a would-be murderer, had nearly killed three times; and the last near-victim
was an American tourist in Brown's Hotel. As mad as Marcovicz is mad, the murderer quickly attached himself to
Fielding for long, pointlessly involved, introspective conversations much in the manner of those Marcovicz is ever
ready to begin with Chance.

Exciting as those events were, nevertheless, some six
months passed before Fielding could find a way to bring
the raw material offered by his holiday, his prisoner-of-war
experiences, and his reading of Waugh and Graham Greene,
which he admits influenced the volume, within the compass

of a novel. He indicates that he made several false starts; but by January 4, 1956, the novel began to move and grow. By the time he saw fit to correspond with his publishers, the work was more than half finished. In London, Hutchinson published it on November 10, 1958; and Morrow followed by releasing it in America on February 25, 1959.

The reactions to the novel were rather mixed. John Davenport in the *London Observer*[1] admired its tightly packed action and Aristotelian intensity. Chad Walsh writing in The New York *Herald Tribune* found it vivid, interesting, and allegorical.[2] Luther Nichols likened it to Graham Greene's thrillers and saw in it much of the atmosphere Durrell creates in his novels.[3] Other critics were puzzled by its structure and theological implications; none saw any connection, however, between it and the other volumes Fielding had published. Father Malachy Lynch—onetime prior of the Carmelite Motherhouse of Aylesfort, Kent, and one of the novel's staunchest defenders—indicates, when pointing out its strength, the source of its difficulty: he calls it a novel of "conscience." *Eight Days* attempts to examine the theological implications of man's relationship to man which Fielding develops on an emotional plane in his other works. He poses the question in this volume which he barely suggests in *In the Time of Greenbloom:* If man needs man to achieve genuine existence in this world, to what extent does he need to relate to his fellow creatures in order to exist in the supernatural sense, in terms of eternity? Fielding attempts to carry to logical conclusions the spiritual limits of Gabriel Marcel's Christian Existentialism and Martin Buber's "I-Thou" theory. These limits he probes in the love-hate relationship of Dr. Chance and Columb Macgrady.

II   Eight Days: *Analysis*

Dr. Chance, one of the principals in that strange relationship, finds himself in a difficult situation. Like John Blaydon, he has lost his love—his wife, who has died; and her death has caused in him a type of myopia of the conscience. He discovers how vulnerable he is to temptations of the flesh, and these temptations and his desire to surrender to them has brought him to the International Zone even though he realizes, as a new convert to Catholicism, that he must not place himself in an occasion of sin. When the novel opens, Chance is in the midst of a disturbing dream, one suggestive of things to come. He dreams that he is back at the prison ministering to the prisoners in his capacity as a doctor; and when some of the men taunt him by calling him "horse doctor," he thinks how much easier it would be to treat them if they were only horses. Soon, however, the sharp sunlight of the Zone cuts through his sleep; he wakes and decides to go to Shibam for some of the excitement he has not been able to find in the Zone. To him, the Zone had "proved to be quieter, less libidionous and more pacific than the confines of Soho, less significant than his prison rounds." In short, it was dull.

During that first day, Chance, much to his regret, encounters Marcovicz, a madman whom he had met as a patient in the prison to which he was attached. Marcovicz with his "great swaths of neck muscles, like ivy round bones," had lost none of his madness and none of his ugliness. Crippled in mind and body, he tries desperately to resume the relationship he once had with Chance. That relationship, essentially confessorial in nature, Chance wants desperately to avoid. He has no desire to listen to the long and disturbing catalog of Marcovicz's crimes and to his disclaimers of guilt. Nevertheless, Marcovicz, like some avenging yet ambiguous demon, pursues Chance, turns up at unexpected moments, and demonstrates his involvement in the turbulent plot in which Chance discovers he himself is a key figure.

That plot centers about Columb Macgrady, an American, and his beautiful convent-educated wife, Anna, who are residents in the Zone. Because Macgrady believes he is suffering from an incurable cancer in his chest, he approaches Chance as a doctor for help. Ironically, Chance soon learns that Macgrady's bodily cancer is more easily curable than his cancer of the soul; for Chance discovers that Macgrady is implicated in the death of his first wife, a woman who was considerably older than he. Although Marcovicz performed the deed, Macgrady, who was in a position to

save her, did nothing. After her death and his marriage to
Anna, Macgrady had come to the Zone in an attempt to
escape his past; he is successful for a while. Eventually,
however, he had fallen into the hands of Fraser, an Australian,
who is the mastermind of a syndicate whose wealth is based
on catering to every possible unlawful desire and whose
safety lies in his ability to satisfy those desires. Macgrady
soon discovers that, through his dealings with Fraser and
Fraser's knowledge of his past, he is virtually a prisoner
in the Zone; for Fraser has taken his passport to prevent
his departure. When Macgrady becomes ill, Dr. Friese,
also a member of the syndicate, ministers to him. Since
Macgrady does not trust Friese, his distrust forces him to
seek another doctor. Only coincidence brings him and
Chance together in the aptly named Botticelli Bar, for their
meeting foreshadows "la Primavera," or spring, for both
of them.

Macgrady senses, however, that something beyond coincidence has drawn them to each other. God, he feels, has
worked His will; for Chance lacks spiritual existence, as
does Macgrady. Like him, whose life is filled with a formal
emptiness and pointlessness, Chance has no direction. A
recent convert to Catholicism, Chance possesses the burn-
ing convictions of the convert, but he lacks the knowledge
of the faith of those who are born into it. Macgrady, on the
other hand, has that knowledge but lacks the spirit. He is intellectually certain of the laws of his faith, but his dryness
of soul prevents him from acting on his knowledge; and Anna,
his wife, partakes of this arid directionless. She married
Macgrady for a cause: she wanted to devote herself to building a stable and beautiful life with him filled with children
and dedicated to his happiness. She is thwarted by his
physical and spiritual impotency. Macgrady and Anna, who
by their marriage have become one being, are clearly in
need of help. This help first comes to them from the emptiness Chance senses in himself, an emptiness he believes can
be filled by sexual gratification with Anna. His desire for
Anna makes him agree to the impossible plot Macgrady has
devised to leave the Zone in order to seek a cure for his
cancer which, he hopes, will be the basis for spiritual health.

Chance agrees to take Macgrady's place in his apartment because he believes, subconsciously, that he can eventually possess her. Macgrady understands not only Chance's motives but also his temptations as the source of his—Chance's—spiritual victory if Chance can conquer them. With Chance's agreement, Macgrady's plot for his escape slowly and sinuously begins to unwind. Chance meets the people in Macgrady's life, all of whom are refugees from convention who have flocked to the Zone in order to build lives they believe to be free. At an intensely senseless and inane party, Chance meets the Sultan's brother through whom he hopes to save Anna should the plot be discovered by Fraser.

Fraser and his cohorts resent Chance; they fear that he will, in some way, help Macgrady escape their influence. When they pressure Macgrady to dismiss Chance, he agrees; and ostensibly, Chance leaves for London. Not Chance, but Macgrady, who uses his passport, boards the plane; and the exchange of identities is significant. Chance has, in a subtle way, become Macgrady; for the world of the Zone once inhabited by Macgrady is now Chance's. Anna is his, but she has become something more than a desirable creature after whom he lusts. His own illness, an ulcerated stomach, becomes analogous to Macgrady's, even to the hemorrhages from which he suffers. For the first time since Chance's wife's death and his conversion, he senses the beginning of another dimension to his existence. He comes to realize that he is sacrificing himself for an individual whom he does not genuinely like—indeed, his feeling is more akin to hatred—yet he knows the correctness of his action. In losing his own identity, Chance, somewhat like Alfried in *The Birthday King*, has gained another life.

This other life grows as he questions Anna. Through their discussions and their fears they learn to understand each other. The days of his imprisonment within the Macgrady apartment and his imprisonment within Macgrady's identity are not placid; they are complicated by Chance's struggle with his carnal desires, by Anna's anger at his inability to act, and by Fraser's attempts to learn Chance's true identity. When Chance's disguise is penetrated, Fraser confirms

his suspicions that Macgrady has left the Zone; and Chance
becomes panic stricken because he must save Anna. He
tries to get her past the concierge, who is Fraser's man, to
the safety of the Sultan's palace, but to no avail. Trapped
in the apartment, Chance and Anna hear the sounds of the
rioting in the Zone which had been rumored for some time.
Added to the noise of the exploding bombs is another, less
clearly identifiable sound. Moving to the balcony from
which the sound appears to be coming, the two discover
that Marcovicz is climbing, ape-like, the side of the building. He tells them that Fraser, for whom he works, has
ordered him to London to force Macgrady to return. Marcovicz, however, fears that he will be arrested once he steps
foot in England and has decided to turn to smuggling diamonds. When Chance persuades him to take a letter to the
Sultan asking for asylum for Anna, Marcovicz is loath to
go until Chance tells him that Magdalena, a prostitute, is
in the harem. Marcovicz, who fancies himself in love with
her, refuses to accept the fact that she, though a prostitute,
will have nothing to do with him.

Chance prays that Marcovicz will deliver the note. His
prayers are answered, and the Sultan's soldiers arrive with
orders to take only Anna. Now, alone in the apartment,
Chance plans his own escape; but his thoughts are inter-
rupted by the sound of a letter which drops through the slot
in the door. From Fraser, it indicates that he is in possession
of Chance's passport which has been mailed by Macgrady
from London. Several enclosures are in the envelope containing Fraser's note, and one is a copy of a letter from Macgrady to Anna telling her that he will undergo an operation
for his cancer and describing his plans for buying his freedom
from Fraser without revealing to her the facts of his first
wife's murder. A second enclosure, also addressed to Anna,
is a telegram from Macgrady's doctor indicating that the
operation has been a success.

Arriving on the heels of the letter from Fraser is news
of Anna's death at the hands of Marcovicz. Plunged into
despair at the turn of events, Chance surrenders to his illness and informs Fraser that he is seriously in need of medical attention. When Fraser orders Dr. Friese to attend to

him, Friese warns him that Chance will not survive unless he is taken to a hospital. Fraser consents to have Chance taken to the hospital not out of compassion but because he believes that Chance alive will draw Macgrady back to the Zone; for with both Chance and Anna dead, Fraser could never hope to lure Macgrady into returning. In the hospital, Chance asks if word of Anna's death was sent to Macgrady; but Fraser has sent nothing because he suspects that Anna may still be alive. Chance wants Macgrady to be informed because of his hope that knowledge of her death might cause a spiritual change for the good in him. Finally, after a long, passionate, religiously oriented argument, which Fraser attempts to counter at every turn, Fraser at last agrees to send the cable in Chance's name; but he also hopes that it will, in some way, draw Macgrady back to the Zone.

The next morning, Sunday and the eighth day of the action, Chance is wakened by the sound of shovels digging into the debris caused by the riots. Elbowing up upon the pillows he can see through the windows of his hospital room the smoke from the houses and churches that had been burned during the fighting. His mind fills with thoughts of Macgrady, the dead Marcovicz, and the murdered Anna. Cutting through those thoughts he suddenly hears Anna calling to him, and she tells him that she is safe at the palace even though Marcovicz had been in the car the Sultan had sent for her. Marcovicz, furious at what he believed to be Magdalena's desertion of him, had killed her, not Anna. Anna comes to the hospital because she has obtained the Sultan's promise to bring Chance to the safety of the palace. When Chance remembers and tells her about the cable he insisted be sent to Macgrady, Anna indicates that Fraser has told her about it and presses him for the reason he had insisted it be sent when there was no certitude that she was dead. Chance confesses that he had it sent because "in a way, I hated him." He did not hate Marcovicz because he was a prisoner: a prisoner, Chance maintains, serves sentence and commits the crime for all of mankind. Macgrady was different, for he had no right to surrender himself to evil.

Chance's relationship with Macgrady was very much like the one he had with his prisoners during his work in prison, for he had wanted to direct and help him. He had wanted to teach Macgrady the lesson of faith by wrecking his marriage, but Macgrady had blackmailed him into performing an act of charity by giving Chance his bride and his despair. Chance had hoped to better Macgrady by his willingness to die for him, but Chance wanted more time. He knew that Macgrady had to be punished in some way if he were to be saved and that punishment seemed to be slipping away if Macgrady were not to learn of Anna's death. "I hated him then with an original hatred, but I believed that because I hadn't failed him once despite all that he had done to me, my hatred was as loving as the anger of God. I had, you see, found my occasion of sin" (369). The cable, he tells her, "like everything else that has happened since I came here . . . was in the providence of God" (370).

Anna confesses that her cable must also have been "in the providence of God" for something had moved her to send a cable to Macgrady to tell him that she was safe in the palace. She takes from her purse Macgrady's reply: "Recovering fast ask for Masses and tell Chance to get confessed before he gets any worse will arrange everything for you both now that I am the new man" (370). Through the silence which followed upon her reading of the cable came the sound of a Mass broadcast over a loud speaker.

Fielding could not have chosen a better ending for his novel or, for that matter, a better beginning. The sound of Mass suggests a wakening from the dream which opens the book. That dream, which Chance has of his work among the prisoners, prefigures his role among the inhabitants of the Zone, which, in many respects, is like a prison. In that dream he is reviled by many and called a "horse doctor." His reaction, as noted, had been that it would be easier for him if they were animals and not people; in that case he would have no need to relate to them on any plane other than the purely mechanical.

This position—the necessity for the healer to relate to the patient—is the key to the central problem Fielding probes in this novel. As a former doctor, he understands the vulnerable position the medical man creates for himself when he does not keep an emotional distance from his patients; and the problem is compounded when the illness is emotional or spiritual and not completely physical. The danger of spiritual contamination is infinitely greater; for Fielding postulates that, in order to cure the spiritual illness of another, a doctor—or any other person—must expose himself to the disease and risk infection. The need to bare the self is paramount because, ironically, that vulnerability which comes from exposure leads to one's own salvation as well as to the patient's. This necessity to risk contamination is especially important when an individual suffers from the spiritual illnesses that Fielding describes in *Eight Days*.

These illnesses he sees as peculiar to the twentieth century, and they are the exclusive property of no particular race or nationality. He apparently diagnoses them in an international zone where all races and all nationalities meet. Ironically, Fielding chooses a madman, Marcovicz, to verbalize constantly the nature of the spiritual diseases which flourish there. He is intent on telling Chance how "free" everyone is in the Zone, but he identifies this freedom as a subtle form of imprisonment because he and the other characters cannot leave. More pointedly, the freedom he speaks of is the very freedom he is ready to renounce: the complete and absolute indifference of one individual to another. This indifference creates a prison for all who practice it—and the prison is so subtle that the walls cannot be felt, nor can the fetters impede save on the rare occasions that emotional contacts are desired. At that moment, the walls become impregnable, the fetters bind and constrain, and the true horror of the prison reveals itself.

The individual himself realizes that it was he who raised those walls and forged the chains, and he also recognizes that he cannot of his own volition save himself because his very act of trusting self and living for himself imprisoned him. He faces squarely the nature of his malady: it is spiritual; and the paradox grows. In spiritual illnesses, every healer is in need of healing; for he can only rescue himself from his prison by losing his own spiritual disease in that of another. He must expose himself to contamination from another and thus secure his own freedom. And, in this instance,

Fielding's concept parallels Graham Greene's in *The Burnt-Out Case*. But the healer must also lose himself in his fellow man. This aspect of the cure is especially difficult for the inhabitants of the International Zone because the first step is to become aware of the nature of their solitary confinement.

Macgrady and Anna sense what the confinement is: it is that of selfish indifference to others marked by sensual gratification wherein the partner is only the source of, not the mutual participant in, pleasure. Such confinement is marked by the loneliness of crowds, by the emptiness and meaninglessness of non-communicative word games. Scrabble is the perfect game for Macgrady's circle and for the sophisticated world it represents: clever language, intricate words, and no real meaning. The words serve as fences to separate rather than join, and language becomes a source of divisiveness, not union. Such language adds to the elaborateness of the rigidly patterned days which cannot hide the signs that truly characterize the selfish: boredom—desperate and never ending, empty and enervating. Boredom is the evil behind every act in the novel.

In a letter, Fielding discussed the problem of evil in this century and its peculiar characteristics. He saw boredom and indifference as the infallible signs of the presence of evil. These signs marked the horrible slaughter perpetrated by the Nazis: millions sent to their deaths not from hatred of them as individuals—there was little or no awareness of them as individuals—and with an indifference that marks the act of a butcher dispatching the carcass of a cow. The sheer magnitude of the evil drained it of interest in the eyes of its perpetrators, for stories of thousands killed brought only a yawn from their executioners.

In the novel, Fraser, the gangster, exudes these two characteristics to the highest degree. He tells Chance in the closing pages why his position in the Zone is invulnerable: he cannot be destroyed because he is needed. This need flows not so much from those elements he supplies which gratify every longing of which the human mind can conceive but from his great indifference to the individuals to whom he acts as entrepreneur for their lusts. This vast in-

difference is reflected in his relationship to Macgrady and
Chance. Fraser cannot conceive of the spiritual torment
through which each is traveling to achieve his salvation,
and neither is he sufficiently interested to seek such an
understanding nor sensitive enough to grasp it intuitively.
He does not hate them; he considers them merely to be
obstacles that stand in the way of some desired goal. When
circumstances remove them as such, his relationship with
them ends; he has no desire for vengeance, not even a wish
to pursue them.

Macgrady and Chance are not wholly free of a similar
indifference. Chance is a recent convert filled with the
love of God yet without the visceral knowledge of a faith
that would take him to its logical conclusion: love of his
fellow man. Macgrady, on the other hand, is a Catholic
born to the faith with the necessary degree of knowledge
of right and wrong, of rules and regulations, which can only
be known to a "cradle Catholic." Ironically, however, while
he knows the rules and patterns of his faith, he has lost what
Chance has not yet found: no pattern, no rule, means anything without human love, which is involvement. Both sense
the path they must take to redeem their lives, but they are
reluctant to take it because the means for their salvation,
each other, they dislike to the point of hatred. This paradox of
hatred in love and love in hatred must be accepted, and the
lesson is a hard one that other Fielding characters have had
to learn. John, for example, is confronted with it when he
discovers that David, his brother, has seduced the girl he
loves; and so must Alfried *(Birthday King)* and Pressage
(Gentlemen in Their Season). Chance and Macgrady come
to understand that one need not be "liked" to be loved,
nor does liking or not liking lessen the necessity for love.

But what of the nature of this love? In order for love to
be present, a mutuality must exist. The lover must also be
the beloved; the healer, the healed. Macgrady is in need of
salvation, but he must also present the means whereby
Chance is to be saved. Macgrady offers such an opportunity
by presenting Chance with an "occasion of sin," a situation
from which evil could flow if the individual so chooses or,
conversely, a situation from which greater spiritual strength

could be derived if the subject rejects the desire to commit the evil. The occasion of sin that Macgrady offers is to permit Chance to be alone with Anna for several days. In painfully rejecting the temptation for fulfillment of that which he craves, Chance gains mastery over himself and achieves that grace—spiritual life—for which he yearns. On the other hand, Chance, as his name implies, offers Macgrady the opportunity to prove that he is "bigger than his sins." The physical examination he receives and the subsequent operation prove conclusively that his cancer is not fatal. By implication, the reader knows that his far more serious spiritual cancer has also been excised. The life of grace awaits both.

This life of grace is similar on the spiritual plane to what John Blaydon is unconsciously seeking in the Blaydon trilogy. Like John, who has lost Victoria, Chance has lost his love, his wife, who, because of the love she had for him, could quicken within him that grace which means true spiritual existence. Chance needs someone through whom he can develop his spiritual life just as John needs someone to help him to establish his emotional existence. Both Chance and John are Existentially dead—they are in Hell, a strange twentieth-century Hell. Fielding postulates that the individual without involvement with another is as incapable of salvation spiritually as he is materially.

It is no accident that Chance, like Dante, wakens from his dream "Nell mezzo del camin di nostra vita." Chance is forty, literally like Dante in the "middle" of his life. He wakens to discover himself in a strange landscape as intriguing as it is disquieting. The Zone, the reader discovers, as Chance sets forth on his journey of exploration, is as much a hell of this century as Dante's was of the thirteenth. Like that Inferno, the Zone is divided into sections, and each is dedicated to the pursuit of its own particular vice. Each is peopled with grotesques recognizable as humans but condemned forever to the prisons erected by themselves by their selfish desires. Their lives are characterized by tedious turnings on the pivots of their sins, which give less pleasure as they grow more familiar until only habit and smothering boredom are left. Lady Zoë, for example, buys her husbands and her pleasures; Robin, her husband considerably younger than she, is enamored of motor cars he purchases by selling himself; Heber cloaks his real appetites by excessive attention to women; and Colonel Tyghe, an English expatriot and scion of a noble family, has tastes for ignorant black women whom he loves to beat. The ironically named Xavier Friese, like his sainted namesake, is most desirous of "saving" people if a sizable profit exists for him; Haleb, the Arab boy, will do anything for money; and Fraser, monumentally cold, indifferent, calculating, controlling, occupies the center of Fielding's Hell.

Lastly, there is Marcovicz. But Marcovicz, despite his great crimes, is not a part of the Zone, though he travels in it. He plays Virgil to Chance's Dante, for he suggests an ideal of the twentieth-century, just as Virgil did of the thirteenth. Marcovicz has committed horrifying, inhuman crimes, but his madness saves him from guilt. Like Virgil, who was neither condemned in Dante's Hell nor saved because he was a pagan, Marcovicz, because of his madness, is neither condemned nor saved. Since he is free of any guilt, he suggests the perfect ideal of this century: he is free to do anything he pleases without stain or taint of guilt. To this extent his situation is attractive, but he is ultimately a figure to be pitied. His madness and the imprint it leaves on his grotesque body prevent him from loving; and, because he cannot love, he can have no real life. The eternal child turned in upon himself, he gratifies his every desire but achieves no peace, no happiness, because he can share nothing.

In this last sense, Fielding takes the philosophies of Gabriel Marcel and Martin Buber to their logical conclusions: only one road leads out of the hell of indifference, boredom, living death; and that is the path of love. Love demands exposure to danger and to pain, but they are the birth pangs which are soon forgotten when one enters into that joyous life of love. The converse, death and hell, on the other hand, are, at first, terribly comfortable states since they focus upon self-indulgence. Ultimately, they are as smothering as the pillow that Marcovicz pressed over the face of Macgrady's first wife.

III   Through Streets Broad and Narrow:
Editorial Problems and Critical Reaction

After the publication of *Eight Days*, Fielding returned
to the problems of John Blaydon and his family in *Through
Streets Broad and Narrow*. The title, derived from the
Irish folksong which wistfully tells of the death of a young
vender of "cockles and muscles," suggests something of
the nature of John's problems in his late adolescence.
Fielding's return to John's story marks a new and wider
understanding on his part of John's personal tragedy. In
a letter to his American publisher (August 17, 1959), Fielding wrote: "As I see it, the John Blaydon theme is intended
at the least to take you through a strange man's moods
through boyhood to death; and . . . through a stretch of our
vexed, magnificent century: mind, place and event, doings
and dreams, foibles and splendours in an unusual but never
unlikely biography of, say, five or six volumes."

To date, only three volumes of this "biography" have been
completed. Nevertheless, in the third volume, *Through
Streets Broad and Narrow*, much of Fielding's ultimate
purpose takes shape; for, through the medium of John's
pain, he commences to draw a portrait of this century and
the problems peculiar to it. The novel suggests not so much
the final volume of a trilogy as it does the beginning of a
roman fleuve in the tradition of C. P. Snow and Anthony
Powell. Fielding, like these authors, sees in his central
character a reflection of his age.

Through Streets Broad and Narrow presented several
problems before its publication in America (1960), not the
least of which was the glaring fact that *Brotherly Love*, the
first volume of the trilogy, had not as yet appeared though
it had been published in England. Morrow, the American
publisher, believed that, as a sequel, the third book would
fail to receive the acclaim given to *In the Time of Greenbloom*. Another problem vexed the editors: the source of
John's trauma, for they believed that his readers would be
confused by references to the disturbing event in John's
past unless he elaborated on it. The matter was a sore point
that arose at a time when Fielding was still immersed in

his medical practice and was burdened with extra responsibilities because his partner was undergoing an operation. Rewriting would be difficult, if not impossible. Moreover, his new vision of the volume as one of a continuing series mitigated against an overelaboration of John's difficulties. The source, Fielding held, was not as important as the presence of the trauma. Furthermore, he could find no genuine reason for summarizing Victoria's death in the tradition in which he was writing. In a letter (September 8, 1959) to Morrow written by his wife, Edwina, but at his dictation, he described that tradition:

Now in England part of our cultural heritage is Stella Gibbon's *Cold Comfort Farm*. The girl who "saw something nasty in the woodshed" is the simple example of every person who has experienced sufficient trauma in youth to be inhibited in later life. In other words, even the simplest reader has sufficient grasp of elementary psychological findings not to be surprised that somebody who has had a shock in his youth, especially one connected with sex, is going to be "lacking in aggression" in his later sex life. This being so [I] did not think it necessary to do an elaborate recapitulation of John's "something nasty in the woodshed" in order to explain the mood of his young manhood.

Nevertheless, Fielding conceded the point, and he developed a slightly more elaborate explanation of the "Victoria thing" and cut later references to it to simplify the connections between the two books. In doing so, the volume developed as a more direct sequel to *In the Time of Greenbloom* than he had intended it to be, for he had originally intended that it would be as independent as *Brotherly Love*, which retains its independence by spanning a larger period of John's life than either of the two novels that follow it.

Other problems developed. When Morrow wanted Fielding to do something about "building up Blaydon's emotional problems in the book," Fielding demurred. In the same letter, he wrote:

In *Through Streets Broad and Narrow* time has absorbed the boy's shock; he is scarred but not blasted. His life must go on, unfold in orderly sequence. He is living on the rather shallow

margin of his consciousness, away from the area of trauma therefore he cannot afford to wallow about in its depths as he did before
he finally rejected the idea of suicide. His chronicler must, consequently, write objectively, cleanly, unemotionally. The 18th
century novelists wrote like this. Therefore, though [I] have not
modelled [my] style consciously on theirs, English critics at least
will certainly see the connection between [my] style in *Streets*
and the style of [my] forebear H. Fielding.

Hutchinson, Fielding's English publisher, raised no such
objections. In a letter (August 5, 1959) his English editor
wrote: "I think 'compulsive readability' is the phrase [which
describes the book] and it is achieved by very few. I finished
the book this weekend and remained enormously impressed
. . . I find it difficult to fault the novel in any detail." No other
comments were forthcoming, and the volume was pub-
lished simultaneously in England and America in May,
1960. With its publication came the freedom that Fielding
sought to pursue his "German novel," *The Birthday King*.
The press reception of *Through Streets Broad and Narrow*
was excellent. In England, Kingsley Amis praised it in *The
Observer*, and Richard Church lauded it in *John O'London's*.
American critics were equally enthusiastic, for *Newsweek*
called it a "prismatic study of a finely gifted young man in
the elaborate tangles of his growth in a complex and wonder-
fully drawn environment."[4] Another review noted it as "a
book of deep emotions, an experience of life, and a warning that no world, however small can be comprehended
easily or discussed glibly."[5]

IV *Analysis*

Like the preceding volumes in the trilogy, Fielding draws
heavily on the events of his own life for the basic patterns
of *Through Streets Broad and Narrow*. Detailed are the
facts of his stay in Dublin, his medical studies, and several
of the people he knew. John Blaydon, now eighteen, has,
like his creator, intended himself for the medical profession.
And like him, he is an individual of literary tastes and sen-
sitivities. John is handsome, intelligent, and self-assured,
on the surface at least, when he arrives in Dublin to begin

his studies. After he has quickly immersed himself in the life of the city, he meets Michael Groarke, a strange, impoverished young Irishman who is "a taker or perhaps, since he never asked, an acceptor." Desperately embarrassed by poverty, Groarke willingly wears John's cast-off clothing and just as willingly accepts his money and his invitations. As a type of payment, and in an attempt to save his self-respect, Groarke supplies John with a variety of information which ranges from what courses to take with whom to the names of shops in which books and supplies can be bought cheaply. More significantly, Groarke serves as a goad to John's flagging interest in his studies.

At first, John is relatively indifferent to Groarke's nationality and to the country at large. As an Englishman, he is suspect and, as an Anglican, mistrusted. Generally, he is unconcerned about these attitudes. Slowly, almost imperceptibly, however, the presence of Dublin, the tangled emotions and mysticism of its people subtly affect him. He falls in love with an Irish girl, Theresa; and through her and his visits to her, he senses something of the land in which he lives. Its strangeness, which Fielding evokes by tiny sketches here and there, weaves a spell over John. He becomes painfully aware of the poverty through the little economies practiced by the Catholic Flynn sisters, his landladies, and by the sight of the hungry, pinched faces of the children in the streets.

The affair with Theresa is abortive. Something of John's past, his love of Victoria, stands between them. More significantly, Theresa herself is a major impediment: "She was a bird on a perch and you couldn't get a bird on a perch." Nevertheless, goaded by his desire, he makes crude advances to her only to be repulsed. Disturbed by his inability to move the girl, John again meets Dymphna Uprichard, whom he had first met in England and who had contributed to his stability in the closing pages of *In the Time of Greenbloom*. His second meeting stirs his memories of Victoria whom she resembles; and since he is drawn to her, he begins to see more of her as his interest in Theresa cools.

Dymphna is willing to accept John's love; but she, in her reckless way, sees no point in giving her attention ex-

clusively to him. Like Agatha Runcible of Evelyn Waugh's
Vile Bodies, Dymphna is slightly scatterbrained but thor-
oughly warm and interesting. Her relative indifference
to him forces John to go to great lengths to impress her,
for Dymphna is a member of Dublin society. John believes
that his friendship with Palgrave Chamberlyn-Ffynch,
a member of the aristocracy and the owner of an all-im-
portant flat in Mayfair to prove it, would impress her. Driving
about in Palgrave's sports car and visiting his country estate,
he hopes, will make her think that he is more acceptable
to her. On one of the visits to Offaly, the Chamberlyn-
Ffynch country seat, John learns of Palgrave's real interest
in him. The visit is eminently uncomfortable; for Palgrave, who is anxious that John's impression on his father
be a good one, corrects John's manners and hurries him
away as soon as possible.

John's striving to assert himself, to prove himself, and
above all to impress Dymphna, whom he believes he loves,
takes various forms: with Palgrave, he becomes a member
of the Ranelagh, an aristocratic club; like his creator, he
joins and reads papers before the University Philosophical
Society; and he even goes so far as to train for a boxing match.
Through all of these doings, Fielding subtly analyzes John's
inner unrest. Musician-like, he counterpoints John's dark
moods and mixed motivations with his external affairs.
These affairs, to John at least, appear to be prospering.
Heady with success and sensing his cleverness in previous
papers he had presented to the Biological Association, he
decides to deliver a satirical paper on the status of Dublin's
hospitals. Unfortunately, his hand is too heavy; and, as a
result, what he had expected would produce laughter, produces anger—especially in those professors in whose hands
his future as a medical student rests. Somewhat shaken
by his failure, John nevertheless sloughs it off by looking
forward to the boxing match which will, he believes, crown
him with success and deliver Dymphna to him as the prize.
His hopes are dashed when he realizes that he has been
played for a fool: the match was planned as a comedy in
which he was to be the butt. When his self-assurance begins

to crumble, the thin, surface ease, that coolness which he had been able to retain up to this point, melts away to reveal the pain he had thought he had finally erased from his mind.

John, as a result, begins to fail in his work. His love, Dymphna, marries an old friend who is in the army. Even John's friendship with Groarke crumbles; for, unable to control the pressures exerted by his ambitions and nurtured by his poverty, Groarke pretends madness and enters a mental hospital. With his removal, John once again finds himself alone without the love of a fellow human until Horab Greenbloom appears upon the scene. His reentry into John's life marks a rekindling of hope, just as it had in *In the Time of Greenbloom*. In this instance, however, Horab has a problem of his own to solve: his brother, Eli, has been sent to Dachau. Through Groarke, whom he has argued into leaving the hospital, Greenbloom attempts to bribe the Nazi press attaché in Dublin to help his brother escape. Dymphna lends her aid by staging an elaborately wild party to which the attaché is invited. The money is delivered; but Greenbloom learns later that his brother has been killed.

When this news is followed by a wild attempt to destroy the Swastika atop the office of the German consulate and plant a bomb, John is jailed for his part in the conspiracy. His release comes too late for a second attempt to pass the medical examinations that he had previously failed. Completely disappointed in love and friendship and crushed by his setbacks in school, he decides to return to war-torn England; and he leaves Ireland without having accomplished anything in a material sense. The darkened ship, blacked out by the regulations of war, conveys him to yet another crisis: the war and England. Isolated in neutral Ireland, away from the mainstream of events in Europe as in a way he is divorced from life by his psychological disability, John has, nevertheless, accomplished the first phase of the harrowing of hell that is the prime necessity in the shaping of a great spirit. John senses the importance of what he has suffered and the effect that suffering will have on him when

he says, in the closing pages of the book, "I've used up something or it's used up me, a part of me that I don't particularly
need."

Despite its plot and its obvious relationships to *Brotherly
Love* and to *In the Time of Greenbloom*, *Through Streets
Broad and Narrow* is very much like *Eight Days* because it
is as mystical in direction but ever so much more subtle
in its treatment. In dealing with a brash, somewhat foolish
John Blaydon who in a foreign country is attempting to
sow his wild oats but not terribly successfully, Fielding
has captured something essential in the trials and tribula-
tions of everyone in his adolescence. In this period in
life, the average individual feels as foreign to his environment as John does in Ireland; elaborate and rather self-
centered plans come to naught; and love means more,
perhaps, than at any other time in life. Added to these usual
ingredients of this time of life is John's trauma, one essentially
spiritual in nature and one reflected in the world in which
he is maturing.

Like John, the world cannot love. Its elaborate plans for
peace, formulated less than two decades before, have come
to naught. In the pictures of the poor and rich in Ireland,
the gathering clouds of World War II, and the political
and racial antagonisms highlighted by those clouds, the
novel represents a metaphor of the need for the relationships among men that was outlined in *Eight Days* —unselfish,
self-sacrificing love. In the closing passages of the book,
John has a vague understanding of his need but the war-
torn world into which he sails has no understanding.

Throughout the novel, Fielding's one overriding theme
is the necessity for love. Groarke's friendship with John,
which suggests the love-hate relationship of Chance and
Macgrady, emphasized this need. Torn by the pain of his
desires and by his poverty, Groarke willingly enters into
a friendship with John that is marked by his interest in him
yet tainted by his hatred for his friend's relative affluence.
Groarke wants to give in this relationship; but his poverty,
he believes, prevents him from giving. That poverty,
however, is essentially a rationalization; for what he must
give is not something material but rather an element with

which he is unwilling to part: his basic selfishness. Groarke, like Chance and Fielding's other characters, refuses to relinquish his identity, his sense of himself, to enter into a true relationship with John. John, on the other hand, cannot understand Groarke's position which stems, like his own, from his early childhood. Groarke's family life has taught him that one gives very little of oneself in relationships with others, and he will not make himself vulnerable to pain which is the beginning of love. John, though ready for love, cannot comprehend how it is to be achieved because of his traumatic experience with Victoria.

His adolescent desire for sexual gratification with Dymphna leads him to believe that love is achieved through sex, and he cannot comprehend that the love for which he is searching is essentially spiritual. However, flashes of the quality of this love come to him at times. Once, John bursts into a rage when the Flynn sisters, his landladies, explain their "silver paper party" to him. The sisters have the children of the neighborhood collect the foil from cigarette packets, and they pay them for it by giving them religious medals. When John is furious because he believes that the children should be given food, the sisters reply: "It's very hard to be finding the words: the *children* want medals." Greta, one of the sisters, adds, "More! They want them more; and the poorer they are, don't they want them desperately?" John is taken aback, for he cannot grasp the point. Educated to believe that material relief is the sum and substance of charity—of love—he cannot conceive of any other need which must be fulfilled. Though he cannot grasp the point the sisters make, it leaves its mark on him. His hunger, like that of the children of the streets, cannot be wholly satisfied by food, by those material things he is presently pursuing: possession of Dymphna and of the good life, position, eminence. He is haunted by the ghost of a pure love for which he yearns. Like the ghost in the song from which the book receives its title, it will follow him singing the same tune until he turns to face it squarely.

In this third novel of the Blaydon trilogy, Fielding employs many of the techniques he had used in the other novels in the series and in *Eight Days*. Essentially, he over-

lays a painfully simple plot with a complex network of themes
and implications which are never baldly stated. His general
method is that of indirection, and the reader must discover,
if inclined, what is indicated or implied. If he is not so inclined, he may remain comfortably on the surface of the
story. Fielding fills his story with characters whose motives,
though recognizable, have enough of the mysterious in
them to make them interesting. He surrounds them with the
sights and sounds of the streets of Dublin and with the
emotional atmosphere of a not so neutral nation.

Again, as in the other books by Fielding, there are echoes
of writers who have caught his imagination. John's inner
turmoil and scalpel-like self-analysis are reminiscent of
Dostoevski's protagonists; the intrigue surrounding the
pursuit of the Nazi attaché recalls the suspense novels of
Graham Greene; and Dymphna Uprichard and Palgrave
Chamberlyn-Ffynch suggest characters in a novel by
Eveyln Waugh, as does the wild party which occupies the
latter part of the book. The structure of the book, however,
is strictly Fielding's. Structure, always an important element in his books, suggests the philosophical atmosphere of
his work: that, despite surface confusion, ambiguity, irrele-
vancies, life has an essential meaning and pattern; that there
is a relationship of all to all. This concept accounts for the
multi-layered structure he has created for *Through Streets
Broad and Narrow;* for, in effect, it is not one novel, but
three.

The first layer, or novel, concerns John's pursuit of love
with Theresa and Dymphna, one which is like some elaborate but comic dance of love that is dogged by disaster at
the moment he seems to be in final sight of his quarry. The
second concerns Greenbloom's tragic attempt to save his
brother, Eli, from the gas chamber of the Nazis. These
two layers—one comic in its implications, the other tragic—
are bridged by the plot of Groarke's struggle with himself
and his poverty. Groarke's tale, which partakes of some of
the comedy of John's and the tragedy of Greenbloom's, il-
luminates the tragedy which lurks in John's blind gropings
after love and the ironic comedy in Greenbloom's elaborate
plans to save a brother who is already dead. Each story

remains a distinct entity; nevertheless, each depends with a delicate balance upon the others; and this dependence produces points of view which affect the reader's relationship to the characters. In the light of Eli's death, the problems of John and Groarke pale into comedy; but Greenbloom's plans are as comic as John's and Groarke's posturings. What Fielding produces here is an exercise in the ambiguities of life.

Greenbloom's story, however, indicates the direction Fielding's succeeding novel was to take. It reflects, in part, his growing interest in his "German novel" which he was eager to begin but which was delayed by his American publisher's insistence on revisions of *Streets*. The episode of Greenbloom's vain attempt to save his brother also reflects an emotionless, objective quality which was marked by Fielding's critics and which is projected in the remaining volumes he has written. His style, never subjective in tone in previous novels, grows even more objective and dispassionate in those passages describing Eli's fate— and this dispassionate quality increases the horror of Eli's doom. It builds upon Fielding's analysis in *Eight Days* of the peculiar quality of the evil of this century: disinterested, emotionless, cold and therefore all the more horrifying. This quality and tone permeate his "German novel," *The Birthday King*.

CHAPTER 5

An Exorcizing of Evil:
The Birthday King

I *The Gathering Storm: False Starts and Critical Reactions*

LONG before the completion of the revisions of *Through Streets Broad and Narrow*, Fielding's letters to his friends and to his American publisher were filled with hints of a new novel which was taking hold of his imagination: his "German" or "Bavarian" novel. His enthusiasm for the new work grew as the restrictions imposed upon him by his medical practice and the revision of *Through Streets Broad and Narrow* weakened. His letters of this period reveal something of the anguish of creative writers as they pick over their material and, with fits and starts, begin the agonizing task of shaping it. The reader of these letters is too often unaware, and rightly so, of the still-born efforts, false starts, and frustrations that the writer must overcome to produce the finished, seemingly effortless product.

At first Fielding had intended to write a play about Hitler, as he indicates in an unpublished letter to his American editor (February 17, 1959). He soon abandoned the idea because he was frustrated by the insurmountable problems such a venture presented to his imagination. His attention was turned away from Hitler as a central, dominating figure in a work to a controlling figure which was never to appear on the scene in one sense but was to be omnipresent in another. Hitler became, in Fielding's imagination, a symbol, just as Fraser was in *Eight Days:* a force that represents the essence of evil in his time.

A play could not sufficiently contain all the implications
Fielding hoped to include in the story that was rapidly taking
shape in his mind, and he turned instinctively to the novel.
Its setting was to be Bavaria, that strange region in Germany
in which Nazism first saw the light of day. Bavaria was
the perfect place because it mirrored in Fielding's imagination all of the ambiguities he recognized in the world:
a patently Catholic-Christian area, it was given over to
Passion plays and piety in the form of elaborate churches,
to religious festivals and woodcarvings of Madonnas; yet,
in the midst of all the piety, the greatest evil of the twentieth
century was enacted there. This juxtapositioning of good and
evil fascinated the author. A people capable of acts of faith
of the highest order was, on the other hand, also capable of
an evil of a depth which makes the mind boggle. Fielding
yearned to trace the consequences of such a paradoxical
state in a people clearly aware of the events, and he selected the Bavarian aristocracy—the symbol of the best and
the worst in German society—for his subject. Since he desired to trace also the growth, results, and aftermath of the
evil, he chose the prewar, wartime, and postwar Bavaria as
the stage for his drama. In a letter to his American editor,
he outlined what he intended to do:

> The book will be about the Bavarian aristocracy living within
> seventy miles of the East German frontier . . . [with their] castles,
> their private chapels and shrines, poverty, *marriages de convenance*,
> romanticism and the mystery of what they were all thinking and
> being when Dachau was as busy as their factories are now. I
> shall find a way to make the strange landscape spring to life
> with its inscape of people and history: the terrible "scent" of the
> pause between Munich and Kruschev with the same hunting
> parties and social junketing going on then as now.[1]

But the novel was to be more than merely a social history
of those terrible years because Fielding had a stronger
motive for writing the book. In another letter, he described
the emotional atmosphere out of which the volume developed:

I wrote out of the fear of evil . . . to this I must add that when we were first married there was an ottoman or sofa cushion in our sitting room and every morning we found on it the trails of a gigantic slug or snail. We brushed it daily; but there it was again next morning. It seemed to me that the night snail had made its trail in Germany for our time and I wished to find it and kill it, to exorcise it from myself.[2]

Fielding began the novel on September 28, 1959; and it progressed more slowly than any other of his novels, except the first, because false starts and deadends marked its composition. The first draft resulted in a manuscript of two hundred twenty thousand words, one far too long for publication; but revisions, difficult as they were to effect, compressed the number to one hundred twenty thousand words, roughly the length of *Eight Days* and *Streets*. Despite many obstacles, the novel was published in England by Hutchinson in the latter part of 1962; and American publication by Morrow followed several months later in 1963. Since the English reviews were overwhelmingly favorable, Morrow chose to quote several of them on the book jacket of the American edition.

B. Evan Owen in *The Oxford Mail* wrote: "For the first time in a decade of reviewing I feel justified in prophesying that a new novel will be judged by posterity as one of the great books of our time." Olivia Manning cited *The Birthday King* as "one of the most inspired and inspiring novels that has come my way in months of reviewing." "Rarely," Anthony Burgess notes in *The Observer*, "is it given to an English author to be able to penetrate so surely into an alien racial mystique. [Fielding's] re-creation of wartime Germany is an incredible act of *Einfulung*. Sometimes we can believe we are reading an exceptionally gifted translation of an exceptionally gifted liberal German author . . . . This is the most penetrating novel yet written about the prelapsarian Teutonic mind." Later, in a study of the contemporary English novel, Burgess wrote: "*The Birthday King* [is] not only [Fielding's] best work but one of the most remarkable novels of the postwar era."[3] Richard Church asserted in *Country Life* that the book had made him "think of such novelists as Conrad, E. M. Forster, R. C. Hutchinson and others who have given their lives to a deliberate exploration of this art of fiction, as did Turgenev. Mr. Fielding has published only five novels, but I have read them with an increasing realization that here is an artist worthy of inclusion in that company."

Shortly after publication of *The Birthday King*, Fielding was awarded the prestigious W. H. Smith and Son £ 1,000 Annual Literary Prize for the most significant novel to be published in England in 1962. In America, in the spring of 1963, he received the Thomas More Medal for the most distinguished contribution to Catholic literature.

II   The Birthday King

The narrative of *The Birthday King* focuses upon a single wealthy mercantile family, the Weidmans, who are Catholic converts from Judaism. In many respects, its members resemble those of the Blaydon family; for the strong Frau Weidman, the matriarch, rules her family as she does its factories. She is blind; but like so many of the blind, she is, ironically, capable of seeing better than those equipped with sight. Since her husband is dead, she, unlike Mrs. Blaydon, has charge of her children. Alfried, her eldest son, a dreamer, is deeply religious and is torn by his desire to enter the priesthood and his need to be at odds with his vocation. In this respect, he is very much like David in *Brotherly Love;* but in other respects, notably in his ideals, he resembles John Blaydon. Like John, he cannot equate ideals with the realities of life, nor can he turn them, because of some psychological inability, into positive action. Ruprecht, the youngest son, is the "Birthday King" of the title; he is life's "delicate child" who is the "eternal infant at his own birthday party" and who awaits from the world the treasures he has been led to expect are his due. He is selfish but only to the extent that though grown he is still a child; and as a child his consciousness cannot extend beyond himself, and the luxuriously comfortable and highly civilized world of the middle class. Though born a Catholic, he is indifferent to his faith, just as he is essentially indifferent to his Jewish heritage except when, in the light of the political situation in pre-World War II Germany, he senses it is wise for him to condemn it.

Understood collectively, the brothers are not so much citizens of a Germany on the brink of disaster as they are citizens of the twentieth-century world. They suggest those aspirations which have troubled and bedeviled mankind in this era; for Alfried's impotent idealism and Ruprecht's inbred, consuming, materialistic selfishness represent, if nothing else, those forces which, on a larger scale, set in motion the events which precipated the cataclysm of the war. Because of their views, the children represent the frustrated ideals of a powerless League of Nations created to end war forever, for it was brought to nothing by the selfishness of nations and the materialistic desires of a citizenry interested only in self. Though Frau Weidman, their mother, the representative of an earlier, steadier if not wiser age, tries to avert the personal tragedies she sees looming in the future for her sons, she cannot. She is powerless, for she, ironically, gave birth to their destinies, just as she gave birth to them.

Just as the brothers, in a sense, suggest mankind of the twentieth century, so too does their Germany suggest the world. The society in which the brothers play out their dramas is as layered with hypocrisy and is as ironically comic as the societies of John Blaydon in his trilogy and of Chance in *Eight Days*. The Germany of the Weidman sons suggests that prisons are built by the individuals who inhabit them; and, though capable of rearing the walls, they seem unable to tear them down. Their inability flows from that defect which Fielding understands as peculiar to this epoch: they lack the ability to love their fellow men—the one quality he stresses so consistently in his novels.

The volume opens when Ruprecht, the young scientist, returns home for the weekend and is involved in a conference of the entire family about which one of its number will control the Weidman industrial interests. Also involved in the conference is Baron von Hoffbach, an impoverished nobleman whose one major concern is to gain control of the family's wealth. For a number of years Frau Wilhelmina

Weidman has controlled the destiny of her family and its business; but because of her blindness and her advanced age, she knows she must resign her position as *Frau Kommerzienat*. The choice of her successor would naturally be the elder son, Alfried; but he is disinterested in the position because he is torn by his strong desire to enter the priesthood and by his love for a young nun. He resists the pressures exerted upon him by his younger brother Ruprecht for whom the choice would naturally mean that he could control the corporation through Alfried. Alfried, in deference to the wishes of his mother, postpones his vocation for two years.

Shortly after the indecisive family conference, Ruprecht meets Alexandra von Boehling, with whom he falls in love. They meet at the Baron von Hoffbach's estate, Schönform, an ironic name suggesting the beautiful formalities of an aristocratic way of life that is increasingly losing whatever meaning it once had in prewar Germany. The Baron, despite the growing meaninglessness of formalities, immerses himself in them and also in the memories of a finer past in which they were a protective device. Such memories protect him from the realities of a world growing more and more hideous because it is motivated by utilitarianism. Yet, as hideous as this world is, the Baron knows that he must become increasingly more involved in it if he and his kind are to survive: he must match himself against the Weidmans of the world, the bourgeois capitalists, and beat them at their own game. He knows that without their money, aristocracy is doomed; and for this reason, he attempts to control the Weidman industrial complex. Alexandra, herself a member of his class, is in a sense his tool in this game; for when he discovers that she is as attracted to Ruprecht as Ruprecht is to her, the Baron is pleased and encourages the pair. But the lovers are soon parted, only to be reunited eighteen months later when Ruprecht returns to the Berlin Institute in 1941. He is able to resume his pursuit of Alexandra when he discovers that she is staying with Carin Baronin von Hoffbach, the dissolute wife of the Baron.

When Carin becomes infatuated by Ruprecht's youth and good looks, she decides to add him to her ever-growing list of lovers; and Ruprecht is equally fascinated with her knowing ways and with her passion, one which Alexandra seems not to possess. The flirtation runs smoothly until she becomes furious with his conduct at an official dinner party; and in anger, she gives an S.S. officer information which Ruprecht unwittingly had revealed to her, throwing doubts upon Alfried's loyalty to the Nazi party and to the state. Her passionate anger embroiders the facts, and she builds upon Alfried's mysticism, which dates from a childhood vision of an angel, and upon his offhand criticism of the regime. Later, that same evening, Ruprecht becomes her lover.

The chapter which follows opens with Alfried's imprisonment, and ironically mirrors Ruprecht's own imprisonment in the sexual fulfillment he seeks with Carin. Alfried is unaware that he is the victim of his brother's apparently accidental betrayal. Because of his important connections, however, his imprisonment is regarded as an unfortunate political error since the regime is not yet prepared to alienate the industrial power of the Weidmans for the obviously mad ravings of one of its scions. Consequently, Alfried is given the comparatively easy position as handyman at the house of the concentration camp's *Kommandant;* and there he is thrown into unwilling association with Herr Grunwald, the *Kommandant,* his wife, and his son, Huburtus. Vainly, the three try to coax Alfried into involving himself in their strange and neurotic beliefs, which—because they are a *mélange* of Christianity, estheticism, and nationalism—Alfried finds revolting. When the Grunwalds suspect that his increasingly more rigid resistance to their proselytizing is traceable to his Jewish blood, they connive to have him subjected to horrible tortures and mutilations to reveal secrets he does not possess.

As the novel progresses and as Hitler's regime is approaching its total destruction, the Baron joins a plot to assassinate the Fuehrer. Carin, meanwhile, in contempt for her husband and in a perverse gesture of despair, takes Huburtus Grunwald as her latest lover. As a last act of hatred for the Baron, she betrays his plans for the assassination to him. As a result, the Baron is arrested and, in a painful scene, is strangled by the S.S. while motion pictures—at Hitler's orders—are taken of his agony. Though saved from the treachery about him, Hitler takes his own life when capture by the enemy seems inevitable. After his death and the beginning of the terror which grips a defeated Germany, the Grunwald parents fulfill their religio-political vision by committing suicide together. Huburtus prepares to join them; but terrified by the prospect of death, he spits out the capsule of poison he is to shatter with his teeth. Coldly, he strips the bodies of his parents of valuables and hides these and other articles of worth in a safe place for the future; sets fire to the house; and slinks away in the darkness.

Meanwhile, Ruprecht, now the head of the Weidman interests, feels some qualms in anticipating the return of his brother Alfried from the concentration camp because Alfried has discovered that Ruprecht had caused his imprisonment. Alfried, however, forgives him and wants nothing of the family's business, nor is he interested in contesting his brother for the position which is rightfully his own. Alfried's mind is filled with the evil, the hatred, the torture he has witnessed; but he thinks that the concentration camp ". . . was the same as ordinary life, but it was speeded up." Ruprecht, on the other hand, senses the danger of his position; he believes the Allies will try him as a war-criminal. He decides that safety for himself and for Alexandra, whom he has married after breaking with Carin, lies in joining the East Germans. The book closes with the realization on the part of the family that it owes its survival to Alfried, whose suffering in the concentration camp has saved it from the evil of the Nazis and from the vengeance of the Allies. It closes without describing the family confrontation, but the reader understands that the Weidmans will once again adjust.

III *Analysis*

The novel, hailed as a clinical examination of the warped German mentality which bred Hitler and the evils which he in turn spawned, is not so much a novel about Nazi Germany as about the chaos which flows from the absence of a deep and abiding love of man for man. It is a universal drama of every man's moment of confrontation and choice between selfishness and generosity, pride and humility, love and hate, the moral and spiritual world. In this sense, *The Birthday King* is not a break in the line of Fielding's novels, though some critics have pointed to the fact that it marks the first occasion wherein he ventured away from autobiography. Rather, the book represents a deeper application of the author's insights into man's condition that were gained by writing the previous volumes. The novel projects a negative application of that principle in which Fielding firmly believes: to live without loving is not to live at all. To this principle, he adds a corollary in this book: to live without loving is not to live at all and is also to invite chaos into one's personal life and into the world at large. Fielding echoes, once again, Martin Buber's philosophy that love brings God into the world. There is no love in *The Birthday King;* and, in the events which transpire, the reader senses the absence of God.

This absence of God is ironic especially in the midst of the Weidman family, the inheritors of two religious traditions both of which are rooted in an uncompromising belief in the presence of the Deity in the affairs of mankind. Despite their Jewish and Catholic heritage, they cannot love. They are incapable of love, as Fielding understands it, because they place their interest in material things before the love they owe one another and their fellow men. They are fully aware of the events occurring in Germany, but they do nothing simply because they rest in comfort upon expediency. The one principle which has ruled their lives and those of their countrymen has been to remain silent in the face of the evil perpetrated by Hitler, for such silence means safety for themselves and for their mercantile interests. Silence ensures endurance to a time when, they hopefully believe, Hitler and his madness will be expunged from the land.

And they are correct. The Weidmans accept slave laborers in their plant, and they conveniently turn their eyes away from this degradation of their fellow men, but their expediency brings them the safety for which they yearn. It saves them despite their Jewish heritage, but it also forces them into a tacit cooperation with evil, that evil which to Gabriel Marcel can lead only to suicide, the last act and the only answer to the comic irony of living solely for material achievements, and the final act of Hitler. Although the Weidman empire survives, its destruction is assured, just as assured as the end of the Germany led by Hitler. And Nazi Germany is doomed because it espouses as a nation the cause of self-interest.

This selfishness Fielding projects in an unemotional, clinical style, for self-interest negates emotionalism in the face of evil perpetrated against others. Indifference to the fate of one's fellow man marks the evil against which Fielding rails, and boredom is the atmosphere in which the expedient works. Since no one really cares, hunting parties can be arranged; glittering social events can be attended; and even a passionate surface allegiance to Hitler can be mimicked. Moreover, Dachau symbolizes disinterest: the ashes of the innocent might choke the throat just as the cries of joy that greet the sight of Hitler shake the sky. Those same ashes might cloud the champagne at the parties or befog the field of vision during the hunt, but no one cares. The lives of those closest to the tragedy are unmarked by it.

Perhaps the sharpest comment Fielding makes against this disinterested expediency is offered in the act Huburtus commits in the dying days of Hitler's Germany. Why should he pay with his life for the acts of a madman? Why should he suffer the agonizing death throes he witnessed in his mother and father for a dead cause? Why not preserve life and as many as possible of those material objects which make life pleasant? He saves every scrap which can be turned into cash later, when the scar tissue has formed over the wounds of Germany, when people have forgotten; his house burns down like Nazi Germany, which it suggests; and Huburtus slinks away into the shadows. The reader is confident that he will return, expediently, as an anti-Nazi in a safer period. Huburtus cares nothing for anyone, and this indifference is his security; but, ironically, his is the security of a prison.

Huburtus has, nevertheless, one virtue, if it can be called a virtue: he is not a hypocrite. He understands the depths of his selfishness and acts accordingly. Others are not so aware of the source of their motivations yet they are equally selfish. Even Frau Weidman, for all her interest in the family, is less concerned with the love she owes them than with the control she can exert. Yet she is an admirable figure; and Fielding's posture toward her characterizes his attitude to all the figures he creates in this novel. He does not judge her, not does he condemn her for the moments when the clarity of her vision is, ironically, short-sightedness. He senses in her particular brand of selfishness an element that cannot be eliminated from human nature if the species is to survive. To eliminate it is to die, for Alfried witnesses such deaths in Dachau.

All hope is gone when this last, vital shred of self-interest is destroyed. Paradoxically, Fielding senses in this self-interest the embryonic form of the love that he advocates, a necessary element if one is to love another. Alfried witnesses the absence of love among the suffering inmates of the camp, for their mutually shared suffering alone is not sufficient to destroy the expedient self-interest that they brought with them into the camps. Their martyrdom, too, is insufficient a price to pay for the love of their fellow sufferers. Since suffering is not the beginning of love, something else is.

Alfried learns what the first ingredient for love is when he begins to suffer himself. He realizes that he cannot learn to love others if he cannot love himself. He begins to learn that all his life he has striven to be unselfish, and this goal, ironically, was the height of selfishness. In dedicating himself to the life of a priest, he believed he could achieve his goal by an intellectual act; he did not realize that love, his real goal, could be achieved only emotionally. To love mankind truly is to love it intuitively. One cannot stand apart and say "I will to love." One can only love through involvement, by rendering oneself vulnerable. When love comes, God comes. So many of the inmates of the prison camp inadvertently throw away their chance to love by guarding their inner vulnerability from each other in reaction to the torture they suffer from their tormentors, but Alfried is more fortunate than they.

Baron von Hoffbach, on the other hand, who is as selfish and as expedient in his own way as Frau Weidman and

Alfried are in theirs, learns that only through committal to others can he achieve the real meaning for his life for which he yearns. He senses that he, the aristocrat, has value for the world despite its denial of the worth of his class. He proves that he is correct by espousing the materialistic goals of those he despises; and thereby, like Alfried, he almost loses the prize for which he seeks. The Baron cannot grasp the proper means to achieve his ideal, but this failure is a common ailment in Fielding's characters: John Blaydon suffers from it, and so do Chance and Macgrady. Like them, the Baron fumbles until events conspire to present him with the proper opportunity. Before his decision to join the plot to assassinate Hitler, he lived in the past and on aristocratic forms and conventions that had seemingly outlived their usefulness. What he failed to recognize in those forms was their underlying value which, translated into the vernacular of this age, could be useful to avert the terrible coming cataclysm. That value was the devotion of the aristocracy to the protection of those of lesser strength than they, to safeguard the ideals of a Christian civilization. As a class, the aristocracy charged itself with the responsibility of upholding the highest moral and spiritual ideals even though, individually, its members may have fallen short of the goal. Material comfort and self-interest ate away at these ideals as the middle class rose to challenge the power of the aristocracy and usurped its place in the world. The Baron is an example of an aristocrat without a cause.

On the surface, he, as a respectable Bismarkian relic of the Kaiser's era, was able to compensate through his alliance with the Weidmans for their Jewish roots. Hence his usefulness to them. He is confident, however, that he, in turn, can use and then discard the greedy Ruprecht after he has commandeered the family empire. In the process of the Baron's machinations, he has destroyed his wife, Carin, and replaced with contempt the love she has once had for him. He has withdrawn himself from life and has involved himself only to the extent that it is expedient for his own safety to do so. Hitler, to the Baron, is a bourgeois clown who must be tolerated until the aristocrats are again in the ascendancy. Meanwhile, Hitler can be useful, but certainly not opposed since there is too much madness in him, too much total evil, for anyone to control him.

When the Baron is approached to take part in the assassination plot, such is his position. Yet something within him, some call from the past, some stirring of his heritage, will not permit him to be expedient at this time. He senses, ultimately, that he will act out of love for his country—a selfless love of which he thought himself incapable. Now, committed, he comes to life. Even in his death, as the motion-picture camera grinds to catch every twitch of his agony, the reader senses that he lives. Having lost his life, in accord with the biblical injunction, he has gained it; and thereby he exposes the lives led by the other selfish or expedient figures in their fullest, ironical, comic dimensions. This, ultimately, is the purpose of the grand life of the aristocrat. In sacrificing all its pomp and luxury for an ideal, the aristocrat demonstrates visibly for those of a lesser station the value of his ideals.

The reader senses in the Baron's death and in the acts surrounding it, the hilarity of the non-committed, the indifferent, the disinterested. The guards who lead the Baron to the death cell are comically meticulous in the manner in which they obey their orders. Their self-conscious solemnity cloaks, but only for a moment, the apathy which is their genuine attitude. They have a job to do; it is expedient to do it well. This creature is the object of their work, and he must be dispatched as painfully as possible according to their orders. But how dull it is! So many have come and gone that all seem as personal as a side of beef to a butcher. But it is their job. And this fact serves as the only defense of the expedient. How pathetically comic, Fielding seems to be saying, that such an excuse can be offered for refusing to love one's fellow man and to act out of that love for him.

In Ruprecht's character, however, Fielding clinically lays bare the anatomy of the non-committed. Like the surgeon he is, he cleanly cuts away each piece and holds it up for inspection and conclusions. Ruprecht, the darling boy, the gifted, the charming, has all that he can hope for; but he must have more. He cannot understand his dissatisfaction, nor does he care to; his only wish is to acquire more in the hope that the more he possesses the more he can attain the peace for which he searches. He will brook no opposition in his acquisitiveness; he will not even permit the rights of a brother to come between him and the object he desires, whether it is love, essentially a gratification of the sexual appetite, or power, the control of the company. Yet he is not totally to blame for his selfishness: he is the product of his age, his station, his family. He will not, however, do anything to counteract his inborn weakness; and his final gesture of throwing his lot in with the East Germans is, like that of Huburtus, the absolute confirmation of his way of life; and he will not change. Indeed, he feels, ironically, that he is the victim. In the closing pages of the book, sensing what the Allies will do to him, he shouts: "Damn those political men. Damn Alfried and von Hoffbach. . . . Damn the Party and the Fuehrer! I did nothing, I neither joined the Party nor fought against it, yet now that I have kept our place for us, it is I who am threatened with political action."

These characters—Frau Weidman, Alfried, the Baron, Ruprecht—as they act and react in Nazi Germany, differ only superficially from the figures Fielding creates in his other volumes. They are as English as they are German. The characters, Fielding wrote, "are all English." They belong to the international race of the lukewarm, the "middle." They are "neither the saved nor damned . . . it is to [this] middle that the prophets speak." They can be swayed to do evil by false prophets like Goebbels with "his clubfoot and radio stations" who subjected them "to the barrage of Hitler's fallen philosophy."[4] Their weakness lies in their desire for "peace,"—a desire that leads, all too often, to expediency with its shifting loyalties and its changing patterns of morality, or to anything rather than committal to a genuine cause, anything rather than face the choice of damnation or salvation.

In the opening scene of the novel, Ruprecht is preparing to leave for his home and the family council he hopes will deliver the industrial complex into his hands. He ironically is in an observatory, a place devoted to clear sight in terms of great distances, for Ruprecht is incapable of seeing to the ends of things. He cannot foresee the results of his actions, which are essentially manipulations. He is a member of the "middle" of which Fielding speaks, neither good nor evil. He shifts about for the correct pattern that will result in the peace he desires; hence, he is meticulous. He senses safety for himself if all is in order before he leaves the observatory for home; he sets about on his tour of inspection, remembering that he must feed the owls. He has but fifteen minutes to do so. This night there is to be no leg of rabbit or mountain hare for them, but a rare treat: live mice. The observatory always kept a supply of them for the purposes of research.

His eyes roam about the room where the mice and the owls are kept. Everything is neat and orderly and in its place. Satisfied, he walks to the window beneath which the "mousery" is kept. It is a charming conceit of the father of one of the observatory workers who, as a woodcarver of Calvaries in Oberammergau, has fashioned a perfect miniature of a Medieval cottage. The frame is carved exquisitely, the little window boxes are filled with paper flowers, and a minute "Madonna of Succour" is poised in a corner niche between the first and second floors. Through the back, which is covered with glass, can be seen some twenty mice going about their daily affairs. For several seconds, Ruprecht is intrigued by their ingenuous performance and he almost forgets the purpose for which he has approached their cage. He lifts off the roof section and selects two mice who tremble in his hands; but his intervention into their world has resulted in an absolute halt in the activity within the cage. Not a mouse is to be seen, none has challenged his intrusion, and all have scurried to safety and the comparative peace of a favorite hiding place. None has ventured to the aid of his companions.

In the large cage in the room, the two owls sit stiffly on their perches; and Ruprecht drops the mice one by one on their tray at the bottom of the cage. Though they do not move, he knows the owls watch every motion of the mice as they crisscross their new prison in an effort to find an avenue of escape. The owls do not look down; the mice do not look up. The first owl, stretching its talons, drops from its perch. At that moment, Ruprecht switches off the light and sets off down the mountain to his home.

His actions, and those of the mice left in their "mousery," highlight the massively monumental character of the indifference to the fate of others which is the singular mark of his actions and motivations and of those of the group he suggests. He does not so much cause evil as he establishes the patterns and the circumstances by means of which it occurs, but he acts out of his indifference and selfishness. These qualities are important to note because Fielding senses in them the greater guilt because they reflect a monodimensionality. They may permit one to be fascinated with the fate of others, as Ruprecht is with the mice, but never to the extent that there is true involvement, just as Ruprecht cannot truly involve himself in the fear or fate of the mice who tremble in his hand. The reader knows that his turning off the light is also an absolute severance of his interest in their end, and this same ability to "turn off" his interest in them is evident in his relationship with Carin, with whom he has an affair: she satisfies his needs, and that is the end of it. There is a type of worldly wisdom in the actions of Ruprecht and of the indifferent, the great "middle," that is characterized by the seeming serenity of the owls, the symbols of wisdom. Indifference, being noncommittal, saves one pain and leads to the peace that is so attractive yet ironically so elusive. The owls are wise in their indifference to what the mice will be suffering; but the mice, on the other hand, are no less indifferent to their fate, occupied as they are with escape. The game which is about to be enacted resembles the larger game played in the concentration camps. The owls in their grey coats and their passivity resemble the guards in those camps; the mice, the inmates. But indifference and non-commitment steel cruelty and make its edge sharper and, thereby, in a sense less painful to those who suffer.

Alfried learns this lesson during his horrible torture. Methodically, the prison doctors set about the task of wringing a confession from Alfried, who, ironically, knows nothing. They become so absorbed in their work that they are genuinely indifferent to the information they are to exact.

Their scalpels, like the sharp talons of the owls, do their work well. The torture proceeds slowly and painfully, almost as painfully for the reader as for Alfried. As days of torture drag on, Alfried senses almost a kindness in his tormentors: "The participants [in the torture] were by now consumed by such intense curiosity as to the mystery of Alfried's will and substance that they no longer had any ethical judgment left. For them he might have been one man or many and Alfried sensed the change at once. He noticed that Halstedt had become as kindly as if he had found him absolved of anything he might have imagined him to have done" (199).

But a change also occurs in Alfried. Each night when he is taken back to his cell he "offers up" his pain to God. Then one day, in the middle of a session, he ceases to feel pain at all; his body seems to enter a "grassy plain in which stood many great trees beneath whose shade he paused at each moment of torture" (300). Alfried's indifference has secured him from pain, but it has sealed him from commitment to the countless thousands of others who have suffered in a similar manner for a similar cause. Once his torturers realize he feels no pain, he is taken from the room and is placed in a ward reserved for important political prisoners to await from Himmler a decision as to his future.

IV The Birthday King: *Grace*

Whitney Balliett, the critic, in a conversation with Fielding noted that *The Birthday King* was not a break from his other books. "Same old thing," he said. "Mother figure and brothers, loving brothers—or jealous of them. Close family ties, ambition, etc."[5] Fielding concedes that Balliett is correct in a sense, for *The Birthday King* is not so much a novel of Nazi Germany as it is of mankind. The Weidman family is based on an actual German family ("He was partially Jewish and she was the daughter of the petite noblesse"); its representatives have the same qualities that he found and described in the Blaydon family which, in turn, he based on his own: "I used them only as a framework for the book: the real characters were all English. I could not see that it would be all that difficult for any race-conscious nation to fall into the pit of division. What I mean is that romanticism is endemic in desperate patriotism and if we are persuaded by it one iota too far we begin to divide people romantically. They are black or white; Aryan or non-Aryan; Houinhounyms or Yahoos."[6]

These characters—Frau Weidman, the Baron, Ruprecht, Alfried, and all the others—are, in the broadest sense, representative of all, be they English, German, Chinese. This representation accounts in a large measure for the similarity Balliett saw among the characters in Fielding's novels. When Fielding speaks of the non-commitment and selfish indifference of members of the Blaydon family or of similar qualities evident in a nation, he speaks of people who are brothers, united by the failings of their human instincts.

The novel, however, was not intended merely as a negative statement of man's expediency. It grew out of Fielding's understanding of grace and its effects on a humanity blinded by self-interest, a subject he explored more directly in *Eight Days*. This element, grace, Fielding defined in a lecture he gave on the genesis of *The Birthday King* at Washington State University. in November, 1967. "Grace," he writes, "is that theological virtue which is at the back of every action not perverse or opportunist." He continues, "And very justly, this story is more about grace than about greed. Each of the major characters has a moment of conviction when his disposition undergoes a slight or even quite important change of direction."

Fielding designed the events in all the lives of his characters, even that of Ruprecht, to permit them a chance to react to the promptings of grace. Ruprecht's moment comes during combat when he and the aviator, Pohl, who is to take him on a special mission, are shot down over the Mediterranean. Ruprecht's first reaction is fury which he vents against the airman for his stupidity. He sees in his own death the breaking of the patterns he had worked so hard to develop, for the Baron would now have the Weidman empire because of the stupidity of the pilot! Nevertheless, when Ruprecht sees the pilot's limp body in the water, he risks his own life to save him. The man is near death, and Ru-

precht tries in vain to revive him. Instinctively, remembering
the formula from his schooldays, Ruprecht pronounces
the words of absolution over him before slipping the body
off the raft into the dark waters.

In context, the incident is fitting. It adds a touch of humanity to Ruprecht's character and is in keeping with
Fielding's objective treatment of his figures, none of whom
is so good that he is not tinged with weaknesses nor so evil
that some good could not redeem him were he to make the
effort. For each, there are those moments when grace prompts
them. Like Ruprecht, Carin responds to the call of grace
when she confronts the long, solemn lines of prisoners at
work in her lover's factory; the Baron's moment comes when
he sees the foreign slave laborers in the rows of lavatories
without doors. He goes about his surface life as he did before,
but from the moment in which he witnesses humanity de-
graded, he can no longer be indifferent. From that moment
he is a conspirator.

Alfried, too, despite his predispositions, must actively
cooperate with the promptings of grace. His time comes
with his refusal to leave the concentration camp after the
liberation. It was, as Fielding puts it, "The moment when he
realized that his life was what he was doing, not what he
might be doing or ought to be doing. It was a sort of conversion from "piety." Alfried had, at last, rescued himself
from his pious desires and engaged himself, through love and
through his own pain, with his fellow man; and he achieves
through action the existence he had hitherto sought only in
his dreams of a priestly vocation. Huburtus, on the other hand,
refuses the promptings of grace; but his rejection of grace
does not spell defeat on all levels, for Huburtus's expediency
will be rewarded. His total commitment to expediency perhaps prompted Richard Hughes to write: "This is a haunting
and terrible book."[7] It is haunting and terrible because, like
all of Fielding's work, it is vaguely familiar. In the Weidmans, in Huburtus, in the Baron, even in Hitler, man sees
parts of himself. Fielding, without comment, holds up a
mirror to man, and asks him to look at his creations; and
what man invariably sees is himself.

CHAPTER 6

Married Love:
Gentlemen in Their Season

I *Genesis and Critical Reaction*

GABRIEL Fielding's sixth novel, *Gentlemen in Their Season* was published simultaneously in England (by Hutchinson) and America (by Morrow) in the spring of 1966. His publishers, and subsequently the reviewers, regarded this book as a complete departure in subject matter from his previous works. Missing from it, they noted, is the semiautobiographical material of the Blaydon trilogy, the Graham Greene-like quality of *Eight Days*, and the controlled hysteria of *The Birthday King*. Replacing these elements is a comic, almost burlesque, treatment of middle-aged men on a sexual spree.

Though ostensibly a comedy, Fielding planned the novel as a serious examination of marriage in an epoch in which few human institutions, including marriage, are held sacred. He approaches his subject—the sacred character of marriage—by indirection through its converse, adultery. The subject, he noted in an interview, "was to be so serious that I had to make it a joke."[1] The gentlemen of the title are two specimens of a breed Fielding considers to be peculiar to twentieth-century England; but like the Weidmans, they have counterparts in almost every country. They are the "men in grey-flannel suits" of a decade ago, who have been married for some years. They are the white-collar workers, breadwinners who also win occasionally at golf. They never actually outgrow their childhoods, wanting sports cars, yachts, and other fulfillments of childhood dreams. Their particular season is autumn, the time in their lives when they have reached the apogee of success and have come to recognize what lies ahead of them. At that time, they notice the grey stubble as they shave; they have collected a little fat financially as well as physically; and they have begun to worry about their health more than their incomes. Their families have been reared; and suddenly, one morning as they prepare to shave off the autumnal stubble, they ask themselves the question, "What have I missed?"

They know the answer, for gentlemen of this type never ask questions for which they have no answers. They miss the innocence and spirit of youth: the quiet time marked by the safety of a regulated family life yet pregnant with anticipation of the good things to come. They miss the things they cherished in adolescence: the excitement that they dreamed would be theirs in a grand passion; the excitement that comes from the imagined pursuit of a beautiful woman, her capture, and the rapturous moments in her arms. Their longing for this excitement grows more attractive as they view the greying stubble and, in retrospect, the patterned boredom of their sexual lives with their spouses.

They long for the excitement of adultery because of the peculiar interpretation the twentieth century has given to the marital state. It has made marriage easier for women than for men because it has taken the drudgery out of housework and has liberated the female of the species from the virtual enslavement that marriage once meant. A man, on the other hand, seems more and more shackled by the need to provide more money and, especially if he is a member of the middle class, to conform. He commutes to work every day; and in a stronger sense, he commutes to and from his marriage. He builds for himself two lives: the married life and a peculiarly single existence. His marriage takes place on weekends when he tends his chores about the house and on vacations when he spends the greater part of his time with his family.

Paradoxically, the woman, Fielding maintains, loses by this arrangement though she is seemingly freer. Through such freedom women can achieve lives in which their personalities can develop, but they have lost that sense of innocence by means of which they bring "goodness into the world." Yet, despite its problems, despite its boredom, its quarrels, and often its periods of emptiness and despair, marriage is for Fielding a "glorious safety," the apt and fitting fulfillment of his belief in love. In that state, two individualities merge; and from the merger is produced a third entity, the married couple, each member of which establishes his identity in relation to the other and in that identity discovers his existence. So strongly does Fielding believe in marriage as this "magical thing" and as a "mystery" that he projects this belief in the basic themes of the novel.[2]

The volume was well received by the critics who generally agreed with the *London Times* review, which noted its striking change of locale from *The Birthday King* and its "impressive journey of the imagination into Nazi Germany, Catholic Jewry and concentration camps." Nevertheless, *The Times* found it "prevailingly ironic, comic, and even farcical." William Ready, writing in *The Library Journal*,[3] praised it for its "style, wit and compassion." Paul Cuneò noted that the novel "verifies what the others have already established: that Fielding is one of the important contemporary novelists." He also cited for praise the novel's "brilliant dialogue" and "apparently endless inventiveness."[4] *The New Yorker* called Fielding a "superior writer" who is "very good, as is his custom, with his low-life figures, one of whom, an ingratiating aphoristic murderer [Hotchkiss], is worth a novel to himself."[5] Robert Taubman, writing in *The New Statesman*, noted in the novel a "hint of Dostoevski in a comic mood."[6]

II *The Gentlemen*

Randall Coles and Bernard Pressage are married men shading into middle-age. The best of friends, they share their lives with each other over their evening drinks in their favorite pubs near their offices in the British Broadcasting Corporation. These pubs serve as their confessionals to which they bring and bare their innermost thoughts and desires, for they hold nothing back from each other. When they part to go their separate ways—Coles to suburbia; Pressage to a flat in London—they feel somewhat cleansed and prepared for the ordeal of meeting their wives. Both are married to women who seemingly lack the sense of ro-

mance for which their husbands yearn. There is a dullness
in the infrequent relationships they have, a sameness in the
pattern of their lives. Neither of the men is completely
happy in his marriage nor is either happy about the growing temptation to adultery, which the two discuss at length
with each other.

The two men are the best of friends in all matters except
for the fact that Pressage is a Catholic and Coles, a humanist.
Ironically, Coles, the atheist, works in the religious broadcasting department of the B.B.C. The fact that he is committed
to no religion or even to the concept of a deity, gives him,
in the estimation of his superiors, that impartiality which
is favored by the corporation. He is, like the Weidmans of
The Birthday King, a member of the "middle," the "lukewarm," the "uncommitted"; and his programs are devoted
to the one proposition that every side must be heard. Coles,
in his attempts at balance, is not adverse to permitting athe-
ists to explain their position. As a result of the blandness
of what he produces, Coles is aware that few listen to his
religious programs. He knows that the "telly" holds more
comfort for the masses than any examination of faith that
he could arrange for presentation. Only the shut-ins, the
hospitalized, or those who, in some way, are far removed
from the worldly interests of the day care in any way for what
he has to offer.

This situation, essentially indifference to faith and to
God, serves as the backdrop of Fielding's story. The comically
ironic situation of a faithless man plying the wares of faith
suggests the hollowness and hypocrisy of what passes for
the life of the spirit in twentieth-century England. Comfort,
hope, a pattern for one's life, are not established through faith,
which carries one to the source of things, but by the "telly"
which stakes out the dimensions of materialistic desire.
By implication, Fielding seems to be urging a rejection of
the blandness of contemporary faith, which has as its mo-
tivating force a desire not to "offend."

But Coles is more than a religious broadcaster and pro-
grammer; he is also a prison-visitor. Visiting prisoners and
ostensibly helping them in some way to adjust to their lives

in prison or to their eventual freedom feed his erotic and criminal fantasies while appearing ethically respectable and noteworthy. In a sense, however, his prison-visiting characterizes his life; Coles, like so many of his class, lives vicariously. He enjoys listening to detailed and elaborate confessions of crimes; he thrills in reliving within his own mind the excitement of the act, the chase, the capture; but he is ethically free and free from punishment. Coles revels in crime, like so many of his countrymen who eagerly snap up copies of lurid stories in lurid newspapers. The delicious-ness of it titillates his palate and gives him a sense of partic-ipation in life that no one of his own acts affords. That life, dull as it is, is supportable because he has his prison, his "telly," to relieve its dullness.

In a real sense, though Coles visits a prison, he lives in a prison continually, one more escape-proof than any in the land. That prison is the rigid pattern of his day-to-day life. He can no more escape from it than the prisoners whom he visits can escape from theirs. He is a non-participator, as are they who feed upon his visits. In this respect, he is kin to John Blaydon, Chance, Alfried. Like them, he has not found the key to unlock his prison door, to free him.

Coles's visits involve him with Christopher Hotchkiss, whose name is apt. He is a "bearer of Christ," burdened with a sense of the magnitude of the crime for which he is imprisoned; but he is even more burdened by the fact that he is not sorry he has committed it. Hotchkiss, for the sake of preserving the sanctity of his marriage, has murdered his wife's lover, Paul. Nearing the end of his term in prison, he asks Coles to write his wife in order that he, Coles, might see her. At first Coles is hesitant; he has never involved himself so deeply in the affairs of the men he has visited. Nevertheless, after much coaxing on the part of Hotchkiss, he does so. The interview is a success; but Coles is not prepared for what he sees. Betty Hotchkiss, as he later tells his friend Pressage, is a beautifully voluptuous woman to whom, he discovers, he is drawn. He continues to visit her, ostensibly to discuss her husband, until even he must admit that he is on the verge of an affair with her. When he talks to Pressage, he hopes to find the courage in his advice that will end the visits to Betty. The talks, however, serve only to enflame his desire.

Betty, on the other hand, while permitting Coles's visits and thereby in a sense encouraging his intentions, is becoming more and more involved with William Smeed of "Westminster Rugs and Pavlova Detergents, Ltd.," whose product is "gentler than feathers." Smeed, though of a lower class, is very much like Coles and Pressage. Now in his forties, he is bored with his wife who, eminently available, can no longer satisfy him. He is attracted to Betty, who presents a challenge that his traveling salesman's heart cannot resist. Betty, in turn, yearns for the seemingly glamor-filled, independent life of her sister, Perry. The younger of the two, Perry describes herself as a model; and she does indeed model between amorous adventures with older men. These men, she discovered early in her career, pay well for the affections of younger women. For tone, she calls herself Bowles-Johnson, not realizing the subtle and ironic humor of the hyphen—the bar sinister which signifies illegitimacy in the family origins. She sends Betty photographs of herself and the "gentlemen" friends from various chic watering places on the Continent.

One of these photographs, which Perry sends from Ostia, sets Betty's mind during one of Smeed's visits to thoughts of her dead mother. He is annoyed by her discussion of the past because he realizes he will not attain his goal with her in that mood. When she talks of her and her sister's childhood, their innocence, their mother's hardships, these thoughts bring tears to her eyes—and fresh frustrations to Smeed's plans. Meanwhile, Coles, unaware of Smeed's attentions to Betty, becomes more deeply aware of his own interest in her. In an attempt to assuage his sense of guilt, he becomes more attentive to Christopher Hotchkiss, bringing him razor blades and other items forbidden to the prisoners by the authorities. Coles also grows more attentive to his wife, Lettice, as if in compensation for his growing interest in Betty. Lettice is rather a controlled woman, and she and her home are impeccably neat and predictable as to the moment-to-moment pattern of her day and her thoughts. Indeed, she is as empty of surprises as are the several parties she gives each year.

Pressage has been invited, as he always is, to the latest of these. The guest list also includes the Foleys, late of Cambridge. Mrs. Foley is aptly named Hera (Greek: "I choose"). Since she is like the goddess, of ample proportions and beautiful of countenance, Pressage is immediately drawn to her; and he "chooses" to concentrate his attention on her. She is wed to no Zeus, though her husband ironically assumes the position of a wise man, and the reader senses that they are not the loving couple they appear to be, despite the fact that Hera is pregnant.

When the food Lettice serves makes Hera ill, Pressage comes to her rescue by taking her out to the garden where she vomits over his shoes and trouser leg. Pressage tries to soothe her; and recalling the pregnancies of his wife, he begins to soften to her. Her condition and her illness make her more beautiful and eminently more desirable to him; and he realizes, as Coles did before him, how moved he could be by a woman not his wife. Inexorably, he begins to understand the dimensions of the attraction Hera holds for him and plots for the consummation of his lust. Despite his interest in Hera, he understands that he still has a deep affection for his long-suffering wife, Helen, and his children, especially for his daughter who is on the brink of her first love. Thoughts of them cannot dissuade him, nor can the advice offered by his friend, Emily Minck, a prominent lutist who everyone thinks is his mistress. In reality, however, she is only a good friend who, like him, is a Catholic. Her arguments against his liaison with Hera are coolly theological and wholly ineffective, as ineffective as the tales of biblical love that his daughter reads and reconstructs in her diary.

Hera falls into the plans of her would-be lover; for she, too, has a reason for the affair. That reason, like Betty's, lies in the relationship she has with her husband. Despite his freshly handsome features, his intellect, his promise for future success, and his artistic and literary inclinations, Hera realizes that there is something woefully lacking in their union. When she has a miscarriage, her husband,

Charles, comes to visit her in the hospital only to be confronted with the fetus preserved in alcohol which Hera has insisted be placed in her room. That fetus suggests the still-born nature of their marriage: every feature is perfect—the hands, toes, limbs—but the well-formed fetus is lifeless. Charles is shocked, but proceeds in his own way to comfort her, promising to do anything she wishes. Ironically, his words produce an effect opposite to that he intended.

"Darling," he says sensing her rising anger, "I'll take you anywhere. We'll move wherever you say."

"Yes," she answers, "Wherever I say. It will have to be *me*, won't it? Originally, I thought our life would have to come out of both of us; but now, there's only me, and wherever we went I should loathe it."

"I'd change," he answers, "I could if you'd let me."

"That's the point. You would; but it would only be *you* changing."

She comes to the point. "I lack a dimension," she said with awful truth, "and you failed to supply it."

In analyzing her own restiveness, Hera also describes the source of Betty's. Hera lacks that same sense of existence, of identity, which plagues John Blaydon, Chance, and Alfried. Though these characters can only approach their problems peripherally, the true source of their malaise is their inability to love to the point where their personal identity erodes into that of the beloved so that a new identity emerges. In Hera's case, Charles is too free with the non-essentials of love; he is too willing to surrender to the whims of his wife; and he is too saving of the inner core of his being. In one sense, he appears to be the overly charitable partner in the marriage; but ironically, he is the least since he refuses to give that quality which would lend the "dimension" of which Hera speaks. He would rather delay, with trifles, the true giving and the satisfying of her desires. Betty is as selfish in her own way as Christopher, for she cannot or will not understand what her husband wants of her.

In a wider sense, the egoism of Betty and Charles and the lack of dimension that it produces is the malady plaguing Coles and Pressage. This dimension which they seek in their extramarital relationships is unknown to themselves, but they are not wholly to blame for the problem that besets them nor are their wives. The structure of life in this modern world has contributed its share since it has forced them to retain their own identities for too great a portion of the day. They suffer from a schizophrenia unrelieved by their short visits to their marriages: they cannot, even when reunited with their wives at the end of the workday, truly lose themselves in their union because, like them, their wives have constructed patterns of their own. These are patterns that permit, as Lettice tells us, their husbands to have their own private existences provided those existences do nothing to break the orderly day-to-day rhythms of the lives of their wives.

Coles and Betty reach out to each other through their sexual encounter; and ultimately, Hera and Pressage do the same in a futile attempt to discover this "other dimension" of which Hera speaks—this other existence which haunts John Blaydon; but something is lacking in these liaisons. Ironically, Betty senses this missing quantity as she encourages Coles; and Fielding characterizes it in an image he constructs. Smeed comes to Coles's house to hint to Lettice of her husband's affair with Betty. He does not inform her because of kindness; like a good salesman, he hopes to clear the field of competition. Lettice is overcome; she cannot believe her ears; she confides in a friend who has suffered similarly, but she knows she cannot follow the advice she receives. She says nothing to Coles, yet he senses that something is wrong: "They lay there in their separate beds as if in separate hives, their heads surrounded by gently moving bees. All was dark; the wind whispered around the eaves and a thin gust of it touched their faces, the external casements of the thoughts which circled and moved continually, turning over and in upon themselves as on an underlying comb of sweetness."

This "comb of sweetness," their marriage, is not present in the relationships that the two men establish with Betty and Hera. Despite the "separate" beds that Coles and Lettice occupy, they ironically are closer than Coles and Betty are in the one bed that they share during the consummation of their lust. The scene Lettice and Coles play out suggests that marriage is more than a physical union; the physical aspects are merely, in a sense, the waxen walls of the honeycomb. Essentially, marriage is the rich sweetness of the honey that fills what is, after all, only a rather rigid container created for the sole purpose of holding the sweetness of life. This sweetness, or honey, or married life is collected slowly and stored away for future use to carry the hive through long winters, suggesting the coldness that has descended upon Coles and Lettice. The figure of the honeycomb also suggests another aspect of marriage not present in the affairs that Coles and Pressage have with Betty and Hera: these are liaisons of short duration, despite the passionate manner in which they are pursued. Marriage, on the other hand, is a slow construction of greater durability, like the hive that holds the honeycomb; and it is constructed to endure the "gusts of wind," the vicissitudes that visit it from time to time. The heat of passion and the coldness of anger cannot destroy it if it is soundly constructed.

But thoughts of the structure of marriage are far from Coles's mind as he pursues Betty. Finally, after many missed opportunities, the act is consummated when, unknown to the pair who are locked in each other's arms, Hotchkiss has escaped prison and is heading directly for his home and reunion with his wife, Betty. Coles is nervous, partly from the strangeness of his partner, partly from his fear that he will not perform as well as he should, partly from his sense that something is not quite right. While dressing, he hears a noise in the house which confirms those fears; and, while Betty tries to calm him, her husband bursts into the room with a drawn revolver. He forces Coles to his knees and demands that he pray the "Our Father" before he shoots him. Shocked, frightened beyond words, Coles fails to see the humor which prompted the demand. Coles, who is forever failing to understand how genuinely funny he is, has no sense of objectivity, which is the first requirement of a sense of humor. He cannot comprehend that Hotchkiss will not shoot him because Hotchkiss does not see him as a threat to his marriage with Betty as he saw Paul as a threat. When Coles does as he is ordered, Hotchkiss suddenly bursts into laughter; the sight of an atheist on his knees praying is too much for him. In a flash, Coles recognizes the role he has been playing; and he angrily strikes Hotchkiss and leaves. When he returns home, he tells Lettice of Hotchkiss's escape; and she, despite his protests, telephones the police.

Meanwhile, Pressage has arranged with Hera to go to France for their affair. The moral arguments against the union have all been examined and put aside, and he has planned a glorious weekend in a sophisticated Parisian hotel filled with the props his imagination sees as necessary for such an arrangement. He has beautifully planned everything; but when he cannot raise enough money, the pair stop at a grubby inn in Calais. Its sordidness more than adequately suggests the nature of the acts to be committed in it. When the lovers are alone in the narrow, cramped bedroom, Fielding's elaborate but subtle joke slithers in and out of the seduction scene.

Hera, the earth goddess, wants more of Pressage than he can or cares to give. Her sexual appetite humorously highlights his age, for she literally depletes him. Young and filled with vitality, she hungrily throws herself upon him; and although flattered, Pressage realizes that her youth cannot be matched by his age. During the long, exhausting night, thoughts of his wife come to his mind: Helen, the personification of beauty and desirability. He mistakes Hera for Helen, Helen for Hera. His confusion further accents the disparity in their ages and suggests dimensions to his desires other than the sexual. His energies depleted, Pressage pretends sleep only to be rudely awakened again and again; and the next morning, he awakens to the sound of church bells. When Hera, believing he is ready once again for her embraces, moves toward him, Pressage gets out of bed and prepares to attend Mass. When she calls to him, he awkwardly counters her demands. Angrily, she orders him out; and when he returns with eclairs and magazines as a peace offering, he finds her cold and distant. She is in the hotel bar, easily parrying the advances of the innkeeper who is as old as Pressage. Pressage is angry but as incapable as Coles of sensing humor and the irony of the scene.

They return to England after a ghastly crossing of the Channel during which Hera once again becomes as sick over him as she had on their first meeting. Pressage learns of Hotchkiss's death at the hands of Peter Caine (the policeman brother of the man he had killed) during a struggle against the police who had come to arrest him. Pressage, knowing of the whole affair through his confidential discussions with Coles and his personal experiences with Hotchkiss after his escape, senses his duty. When he tells Coles that he plans to attend the funeral, Coles demurs; for he has patched up his quarrel with Lettice, just as Pressage has with Helen, and is in no mood to open old wounds. He has come to realize the comfort of marriage and will not jeopardize his again. Lettice, he insists, will send a wreath. Pressage, on the other hand, feels impelled to go. He realizes that, in some way, Hotchkiss has paid the full price for the sanctity of his home—a price neither he nor his friend Coles has paid though each was in the act of destroying the union which is his only support. Hotchkiss becomes, in a sense, the scapegoat. The aptness of his name, Christopher, is more apparent at the funeral, which is also attended by Barshnell, his friend from prison who also has killed for his marriage. Of them all—Coles, Pressage, Barshnell, Hotchkiss, even Smeed—only Hotchkiss, who believed in the sanctity of marriage, has paid the full price.

With Pressage at the funeral is Helen, who has forgiven him; Emily Minck, who has entered into an alliance with her; and Cecily, his daughter whose mind is filled with thoughts of love. Also attending are Betty and Perry, but they leave before the interment. During the ceremonies, Pressage's mind wanders over the past, and Cecily's is drawn to the future. Betty, who nervously occupies a back pew, wants desperately to leave. Not a Catholic, she feels out of place and ill disposed. Returned home, she discovers that an elaborate tea has been prepared. Wanting none of it, she nevertheless listens patiently to the advice about her future given by her sister and a neighbor. After they leave, she receives a visit from Smeed with the same thought in mind but with little hope of success in the light of the day's events. Betty, indifferent to him, permits him to begin his rather humorous courting of her and ultimately she gives in. He prides himself on accomplishing in half an hour what he could not previously achieve in a whole evening.

After the funeral, Pressage, Helen, Emily, and Cecily return to London. Emily has promised to treat them all to dinner, but Cecily refuses to go. Cecily wants to return to her room to work on her "Great Love Stories" based on the Bible; but back in her room, she cannot decide which biblical story to choose. Her indecision ends when her Bible, as she leafs through it, opens to the story of Tobias and Sarah. Sarah, the story goes, was married seven times to men whose only thoughts were of possessing her body; and each had died on the first night of the honeymoon. When she was to wed Tobias, everyone predicted a similar fate for him. But an angel had instructed Tobias that he was to have no relations with his wife for three days, and these days were to be set aside for prayer to God and for their union with Him. Tobias prayed, "We come of holy lineage; not for us to mate blindly, like the heathen that have no knowledge of God." And Sarah prayed, "Have mercy on us, Lord have mercy on us." Outside, the men waited in vain beside the open grave they had dug for the body of Tobias.

III *Analysis*

It is fitting for Fielding to end his novel with the story of Sarah and Tobias as related by Cecily. Cecily, at the dawn of maturity and on the brink of the love for which she yearns, serves as a counterpoint to the tired passions of her parents, of the Coles, and of the young couple with their infant who have moved next door and whose quarrels Cecily can hear. She suggests the beginning of a new and hopefully wiser cycle of life. She senses the joys that await her—the encounter with the man who is to be hers for the remainder of her life, be he a handsome workingman, like the youth she sees on a bus, or a guardsman tall and virile in his polished boots and tight-fitting uniform; the marriage; the nights of love; the children; and the days filled with joy.

Her interest in the love stories of the Bible is important. It suggests that she will have sounder foundations for her marriage than that of her elders who, like the seven husbands of Sarah, have seemingly forgotten the true basis for marriage. It is not, as they learn to their sorrow, "mating blindly" like the "heathen"; it is something far more directed, far more holy, and far more permanent.

But for all of Cecily's seriousness in pursuit of love, her comic approach is Fielding's method in the novel: the underlying seriousness of his intent is buoyed by the comic implications of the situation. This humor laces each of the liaisons he presents, and the comic comes close to burlesque when Smeed courts Betty and each move he makes against the citadel of her resistance is directed in asides by selections from his manual on salesmanship. When Smeed wants desperately to press home to his goal, but is countered by Betty's desire to talk, he recalls the manual's injunction to control his haste: "Though the good representative is always in a hurry, he never appears to be. He knows that although time is money, there's plenty of it" (47).

When Betty goes on talking about her dead mother and the love she withheld from her, Smeed's thoughts turn to his own family: to his wife and son Charlie who would have made a good male nurse but chose the more lucrative world of business. When he is shaken from his thoughts by Betty's remarks on death and is certain he has lost his advantage, a passage from his manual again comes to his rescue: "Bereavement need not spell No Sale. Give what comfort you can and remember that gratitude, though not immediate, is often inevitable." He decides not to give up and continues his pursuit; when Betty begins to cry, however, he realizes that all he will get that night is tea. "Never acknowledge defeat," the manual cheerfully advises. "There is always another time."

The interjection of aphorisms from Smeed's salesman's manual is apt irony. What he is attempting is a sale as shoddy, in a sense, as any he perpetrates for a living. He is as disinterested in the product he is attempting to sell Betty as he is in the rug-cleaning preparation he peddles which interests him only in so far as he is able to support himself and his family with the money coming from its sales. The product he is displaying to Betty serves an analogous purpose: its sale supports the ego of a man in his forties when doubts about his virility and when his falling hair begin to plague him. If he overcomes Betty's sales resistance, he achieves the currency that will support his belief that he is the man he always was. He cannot afford to lose the sale; it means too much to him.

The seriousness that underlies what is essentially a recasting of the "traveling salesman" joke is also reflected in the scene in which Coles nears the consummation of his desires. Coles congratulates himself on the fact that his knees are remarkably steady as he begins the seduction scene. His moving through, step by step, the elaborate ritual, which for a younger man is easier, more natural and admirable, becomes hilarious. A constant comparison between Betty and Lettice runs through Coles's mind as he proceeds with the affair: he thinks of his courtship, his first kiss, his honeymoon; he makes mistakes with Betty, he becomes embarrassed, he fumbles. Yet, all the while, he never falters in his desire to continue the charade. Betty, in this scene, becomes for Coles what she means to Smeed. She is an object to be conquered not for herself, but to be possessed rather for what that possession means to the man—a renewal of belief in himself, a seeking for reassurances that, after all, he is not in the autumn of life, that a new, more attractive spring awaits him. In reality, all he genuinely wants is the wife about whom he constantly thinks.

Like Coles and Smeed, Pressage is involved in a scene that is hilariously funny in one respect but devastatingly serious in another. When the scene opens, the reader discovers Pressage awake, exhausted, on the narrow bed in a cheap French boardinghouse. The bedsprings twang "like an old-fashioned cash register every time he moved." The connection between Smeed's act and his is clear: the sound makes "an effective accompaniment to his thoughts." Those thoughts, like Smeed's manual, are filled with the mistakes he had made in his affair with Hera. First, he should have borrowed enough money to take Hera farther than Calais—to a location more conducive to love-making, to Paris, a sophisticated hotel, to champagne and caviar and all those elements the dreamer senses should surround passionate love. Second, he should have had the "guts" to forget his religion.

Ironically, he has. For all his thoughts of the prohibitions of his faith against what he is doing, he has, nevertheless, gone through with his plans. Third, he should have realized that Hera was not greatly interested in him. That, too, smacks of irony. He refuses to understand that he is as uninterested in her as she is in him. Both use each other in an attempt to achieve what they sense they lack. As Coles thinks of Lettice, Pressage thinks of Helen. The fulfillment he seeks in Hera can, with a slight adjustment of sights, correcting his moral myopia, be better satisfied in Helen. It is Helen he wants all through the comic sexual struggle with Hera, who drains him rather than fulfills him. In his own way, he is as impotent with her as Coles is with Betty. It is an impotency which robs the affair of satisfaction.

Coles and Pressage, who unlike Smeed, are essentially gentlemen, sense that there is no future in their relationships with these women. As their affairs begin in earnest, they long to be free to return to their marriage partners who represent something stronger than a desire to stay the ravages of time. Their wives represent continuity, stability. What the men cannot fully realize is that the continuity, the structure marriage gives to life, cannot be transmitted nor lived on the basis of past relationships; for Lettice and Helen in their forties are not the Lettice and Helen they had courted and married—just as Coles and Pressage are not the men they were when they were twenty. The couples must adjust and readjust the basic patterns of their lives: they must mingle the patterns of their separate lives to achieve once again the honey which is the source of a live and vital marriage.

In a key scene, Coles comes to realize this great need for constant readjustments in his relationships with Lettice, as well as her responsibilities to do as he does. He senses that she must come to live with the memory of his affair with Betty. As with the scenes previously described, his affair is fraught with comic implications but is essentially serious in purpose. Lettice's feminine intuition tells her that Coles has had sexual relations with Betty on his return from the affair, and his attempts to appear natural are weak and unconvincing. The confrontation scene is played with all the surface comic conventions of such scenes: the irate wife who knows "all" bitterly reveals that knowledge as a weapon to reduce the erring spouse to submission; the confused, guilty husband, vainly defends himself against the unstaunchable torrent of argument. Conventional, yes, but only on the surface. When Lettice, in her anger, drops the Wedgwood bowl of potpourri, the dead flowers suggest their life together; and the reader senses that the shattering of the pottery signifies the shattering of something even more fragile, the shattering of the cocoon woven about their relationships. What will emerge from this honest re-action to Coles's transgression is a more genuine marriage, a clearer recognition of what they are and what they mean to each other; but this result will not come without struggle and pain, just as the emergence of the butterfly from its chrysalis is not effected without difficulty. Beautiful as that bowl was and fragrant as its contents were, Coles recognizes that Lettice and he "were buried together in there beneath those eternal flowers" and that now, from the "potpourri something had been resurrected" (222).

Though Fielding's treatment of sexual impropriety is essentially comic, he does not advocate evil. Through a subtle and inventive arrangement of events which flow naturally from the personalities of his characters comes the suggestion that the Deity permits his creatures to traffic in evil if they so choose; but he does so to help them to apprehend the good toward which they ought to direct themselves. This same permissiveness is present in Fielding's other volumes; and like the characters in those novels, Coles and Pressage have lived only partially, caught as they are in the patterns of a life not entirely of their own creation. The richness of the lives they could lead in their marriages is only partially visible to them, but the shock that comes from the consummation of their lustful desires awakens them to the good life. The whiteness of white cannot be fully understood on a human plane without the presence of the blackness of black—or so Fielding implies.

Technically, the novel is reminiscent of the five preceding it; for it is as elaborately designed as a formal ballet. Undisciplined though it may appear on the surface, the reader

senses the control upon which it is based. Its structure consists of a richly textured pattern that is formulated by the relationships of Coles to Pressage and, through them, the
relationships with the remaining characters. Coles and
Pressage suggest two sides of a single character: the one,
Coles, formal, materialistic, relatively unbelieving; the
other, Pressage, sensitively tuned to a belief in God, yet
incapable of living up to those ideals postulated by his
beliefs.

All of Fielding's novels contain a similarly related pair
through whom the patterns of each novel originate and on
whom they are based. *Brotherly Love* has David and John;
In the Time of Greenbloom, John and Victoria; *Through
Streets Broad and Narrow,* John and Groarke; *Eight Days,*
Chance and Macgrady; *The Birthday King,* Alfried and
Ruprecht. Each pair, like Coles and Pressage, suggests
two aspects of a single personality which demand a resolution of their diametrically opposed ideals. The only resolution is love—love that erases differences, that merges
individualities. John and David suggest man's basic desire
to follow an ideal (John) but only to be thwarted by natural
drives and instincts (David). John and Victoria, on the other
hand, imply man's need to learn the basic patterns which
precede true love between man and woman, and the consequences that occur when such patterns are disturbed in
youth. John and Groarke suggest the need for love, which
can only be discovered when one loses the sense of self.
Chance and Macgrady learn that they have no hope, even
though they do not like each other, without an unselfish
sacrificing, spiritual love. The need for a sense of brotherhood based on a true understanding of the love out of which
it must spring is accented in the relationships of Alfried to
Ruprecht. Coles and Pressage suggest a frame for the picture of love and its variations which Fielding has been
constructing in his novels. In many aspects, they reflect
all of his characters at middle age. They reflect what occurs
when all these interests are focused in individuals who
sense that their lives are declining, that their autumn will
give way to winter, and that their winter will bring with it
death, that final resolution to all their problems.

CHAPTER 7

The Significance of Gabriel Fielding

I *Literary Theories*

COMMENTING on a deeply moving first novel of a close friend of the family (Catherine Dupré's *The Chicken Coop*), Gabriel Fielding wrote, "I think of the novel as a mourning, an experience so real and deeply felt by the writer that it reaches the reader with a kind of primitive innocence and power." This statement, though an accurate description of Mrs. Dupré's book, is more applicable as a definition of Fielding's credo of the novel. The indication that personal experience and pain are sources of effectiveness, however, is not new to the novel for most writers seek data from their own lives to flesh out their plots or characters. But Fielding refers to something more than personal experience; he speaks of personal experience that moves out to the reader and touches him "with a kind of primitive innocence and power"—words that call for closer examination. Superficially, they suggest the intensity of the experience depicted and of the pain described; but they also indicate the medium through which this experience and pain are transmitted. Fielding is not concerned with a transmission to the intellect; he hopes to reach and move an aspect of man which, though elemental, is essentially more honest and less capable of delusion.

The words suggest that Fielding believes that what is sensed in certain instances is so much more valid, more moving than data carefully gathered and processed by the intellect. Suggestion is more compelling than bald statement; indirection opens the reader to wide vistas; definition confines him to a narrow vision. All these beliefs produce in Fielding's works an elusiveness noted by so many of his critics. This elusiveness, in turn, develops into an

[136]

attractive demand that he makes upon his reader to enter
into his novels, to contribute his own parallel experiences,
to participate, so to speak, in their creation—in short, to
permit the reader to recognize the novel as something not
apart from his own real world.

These demands that he makes and the primitive appeal
that they present produce certain important effects on
Fielding's art. Primarily, they result in a horror of an over-
intellectualized approach to the writing of novels. In a
critical essay, "Sex, Symbolism and Modern Literature,"
he recoils when commenting upon Joyce's conscious use
of symbolism and allegory in *Ulysses:* "James Joyce in
The Dubliners showed himself to be a master of story telling
but in *Ulysses*, magnificent as it is, he allowed his learning
and the symbolism of Leopold Bloom's twenty-four-hour
odyssey to overwhelm his clarity. Any good novel, it has
been said, is 'trying to be a poem' and, as Robert Frost
wrote, 'A poem like ice on a hot stove, should ride on its
own melting.' By forcing his novel to conform to Homer's
Odyssey, Joyce seems to have sacrificed some of his own
'inner necessity' and thus limited its appeal."[1]

Fielding mistrusts consciously applied symbolism for
other reasons than its effects upon the novelist whose
"inner necessity" may be sacrificed to the destructive and
constrictive demands of such a device. That "inner necessity" is essentially the "experience so real and deeply felt
by the writer" of the quotation that opened this chapter, and
he mistrusts symbolism because he fears that it may "lead
to over simplification."[2] Life, as Fielding understands it
and projects it through his novels, is complex; and such
complexity does not lend itself readily to definition in terms
of artificially selected and contrived symbolism and allegory.
Furthermore, the result of the application of such devices
is often a "perversion of meaning" because their essential
appeal is to the intellectual desire to arrive at neat and
orderly understandings rather than to the emotions, which
are unconcerned with neatness and order.

Above all, Fielding mistrusts those devices because, when
applied consciously, they deprive "their subjects of subtlety
and freedom," two qualities of the novel that he prizes.

He fears too direct a control because he senses in that control a curtailment of the reader's imagination and of his ability to respond emotionally and personally to the novel's "primitive innocence and power." Fielding conceives the novelist's relationship to the characters he creates and the reader who responds to them to be analogous to those relationships of the Creator to His creatures. Like God, who has created man and given him a will free to explore and determine his own life, Fielding believes that the novelist is compelled to give his creatures and his readers a similar freedom. Consciously applied stylistic devices are capable, he concedes, of "enriching literature," but they smack too much of unnatural control.

His fear of such control and of its ability to throttle a work of art proceeds directly from the fundamental understanding he has of his personal role as a novelist. This role he considers so important that he boldly states "Where science fails, the intuition of the artist may sometimes succeed. . . ."[3] He speaks here of guilt complexes which he believes are the sources of so much mental illness today and of the inability of science to discover their causes and to illuminate their "origins." To imprison the artist's intuitive ability to reveal truths so necessary to mankind is to pervert the very nature of the art that the individual practices. Consciously applied literary decoration is a perversion that destroys "that spontaneity which is essential to a good work"; it does so to the point that the writer can produce "symbols [which are] so easily minted that the counterfeit can unintentionally fake the instinctive knowledge of real writers. [By such means] second-rate work may be made to seem so significant that for a time it may mislead even astute critics. For symbolism and allegory, even in clumsy hands, give a kind of elegance and shape to a story. But before long the dull progression they impose induces the kind of boredom we experience when we read a fairy story."[4]

Moreover, the products of such a "counterfeiter" are detrimental to art because they destroy the true purpose of art and, ultimately, the artist himself. These products blur and ultimately obliterate the "inner necessity" which moves the artist to write. Conscious counterfeiting produces a sophistication that strikes at the one element in the nature of the artist which nurtures this "inner necessity" to create. It destroys that quality he can ill afford to lose if he is to remain an artist: his "permanent adolescence" —the fundamental well-spring of his art. It is his "sense of wonder, his ability to speculate, his freshness and daring."[5]

His "permanent adolescence" is that element which permits the artist to adhere to the function of the novel. For Fielding, the novel's function is "only a bit lower than prophecy and poetry."[6] Without a strict adherence to this function, Fielding maintains that an author "will never be read." As for what this function is which is "only a bit lower than prophecy and poetry," the answer lies in his definition of the responsibilities of a novelist. The novelist "must entertain . . . to illuminate whatever he is writing about. This is the poetic function of the writer . . . next . . . is to instruct by sympathy. One of the loveliest things about this is when you say or feel, 'Ah, I too knew this. I knew it without knowing it, but now I know it. . . .' In short, the writer must reconcile himself and life."[7]

Entertainment and illumination are, then, the responsibilities of a function which is "only a bit lower than prophecy and poetry." First, the novelist must entertain before he attempts anything else; second, but a very close second, he must instruct the reader in truths which heretofore the reader apprehended only intuitively. When Fielding speaks of instruction, however, he does not mean overt propagandizing. He insists rather that the novelist calls forth, as Christ called Lazarus from the tomb, truths which lie buried and seemingly dead in the reader. In this sense, the artist is a revivifier, a diagnostician rather than a healer. He must serve as the eyes of humanity who "seeing have not seen."

But there is an injunction in Fielding's concept which demands that the artist must not force sight by artificially contrived metaphor or by tawdry allegory. If the reader refuses to see, it is his right. The artist should persuade the reader to apprehend the truths he presents by means of "sympathy." Ultimately, instruction in the truths of life is possible only if the artist is capable of producing a work in which the experiences depicted stir the sympathies of the reader by their genuineness. This sympathetic instruction leads to a clear and specific end. The writer must instruct his readers in those truths which "reconcile" them to "life." He operates, then, with the express intention of helping his readers to achieve a *modus vivendi* in a world which is essentially incompatible.

To all of this, Fielding adds a third point: "the final function is . . . his [the artist's] insistence upon being a wise man—asking a wise question."[8] The artist must progress in his knowledge of life, in his experiences, in his search for those ultimate truths which lie hidden within all men. These truths must be discovered if the artist is to fulfill his function and if the reader is to achieve some sense of stability in his life. This point of progress calls for additional clarification of the quotation cited at the opening of this chapter. When Fielding speaks of that quality of Mrs. Dupré's work which most attracted him, he speaks of a "mourning." This element is the key to the necessary progress and ultimately to the truths he demands that the novelist reveal. For Fielding, mourning is an act filled with pain.

In conversations with the author, this subject of pain was a recurring theme in various contexts. In a published interview, he once stated, "I write out of pain—I believe most writers do."[9] Superficially, the statement could be construed to mean the more obvious pains associated with the act of creation wherein the artist searches for the language which gives life to his ideas, but Fielding's understanding of pain is deeper and more significant for his art. This deeper meaning refers to "mourning," which is essentially the pain of loss: the agonizing awareness which one once possessed (never material things) but no longer has, which is intensified by a passionate yearning for its return, be it innocence, youth, love, ideals. This intensely disturbing pain, if effective in revealing truths to the reader, must be directly and vividly experienced by the writer. That element is the only element that will stir the reader's sympathies because such pain has touched all of humanity.

Pain serves yet another purpose. In addition to animating

the author by giving him the power to stir the sympathies of his readers, it serves as the principal source of that quality which makes the author's work worthy of publication. That quality is "obsession." Fielding states: "I think that the writer who is most worthy to be read is the writer absolutely and totally obsessed with what he has to say. He is not writing from mere fantasy of fruitless frustration, he's writing from obsession."[10] The writer must, nevertheless, control this "obsession" in some manner if he is to direct it to the fulfillment of his functions as a novelist.

This control of his "obsession" must come from a concentration of the writer's energy. According to Fielding, "The energy [of a writer] must be so concentrated that the writer will achieve enormity out of the narrowness and perfection of his obsession."[11] That this "enormity" must be achieved, Fielding believes intensely. If not achieved, then he cannot help his readers apprehend through "sympathy" the truths of life buried within each of them. In other words, if the writer does not achieve universality of appeal, he fails in his vital function, no matter how obsessed he is with pain. He is unsuccessful because his pain is too personal and thereby too obscure to elicit sympathy and the feeling of the reader that he has suffered in a similar way. The reader becomes a distant, objective observer rather than an involved, subjective sufferer. Obsession alone, therefore, is not sufficient to reveal truth sympathetically. As for the method that helps the artist channel the "obsession" in order to produce the necessary "enormity" of appeal, Fielding's answer is "intuition."

In discussing the processes of writing, the author chanced upon the problem that confronts all writers at one time or another: the lack of the exact language to carry their ideas. Fielding never directly concerns himself with the problem of language; instead, he concentrates upon the meaning he wishes to convey. The words, he reports, follow intuitively. As an example, he relates the story of how, at a point in one of his novels, he was troubled in his search for the right words. He retired to bed disturbed by his inability to discover them only to awaken at two in the morning with the words crowding his brain. As he explained, "I know that when I'm writing well I have a feeling of having come into my own, everything seems justified."[12]

He plans his work to a degree but never to the point where his intuition could cease to function or where he could be fully aware of precisely what he will write: "Writing to me is a voyage, an odyssey, a discovery, because I'm never certain of precisely what I will find."[13] Consequently, because of his method and his firm belief in the intuitive process, he writes that "spontaneity . . . is essential to good work."[14] Contrivance of any type is an enemy of this "spontaneity" and especially so is the almost universally employed contrivance he so very much deplores in serious contemporary writers: the conscious application of other "meanings" to their work. "I don't much care for symbolism," he asserts, "not because I am too much concerned with it, but because as a writer, I have never consciously used it . . . it is worthwhile considering which is more important: the thing or the symbol behind it."

He is also keenly sensitive to another contrivance which limits the workings of intuition, one, perhaps, even more deplorable than contrived symbolism. This device is the startling and inventive vocabulary which primarily calls attention to the ingenuity of the writer and only secondarily contributes to the forward movement of the story or to the truth of the statement. In one discussion, Fielding adversely criticized a popular author who used in one of his novels the unfortunate phrase "constipated constellation." This tendency—the overweening desire to create memorable phrases —Fielding has observed in many serious contemporary writers, and it has caused him to turn away from their novels. But above all, Fielding's dislike of contrivances indicates more forcibly his personal predilection in his own work for spontaneity and for the intuitive aspects of creativity.

But what of these "truths" which must be conveyed "sympathetically" and "intuitively" through an intensely felt "experience"? Of what do they consist? Through what thematic material are they to be apprehended? Fielding once noted that the "most important part of living is loving."[15] Through his exploration of the facets of human and Divine love, he hopes to reveal the truths that he considers his duty to reveal. Because love is one of man's most primitive, as well as one of his strongest and most controlling, emotions, Fielding senses that it can best serve his purposes in the novel.

During a conversation, he underscored the importance of love as a theme in literature. The author noted its prominence in all periods, even in the Victorian age, despite the conventional restrictions that period imposed upon discussions of its more sordid aspects. Fielding admitted that *Wuthering Heights* is one of his favorite books and one that inspired *In the Time of Greenbloom* in part. He noted that Catherine Earnshaw and Heathcliff were emotionally and intuitively drawn to each other and would have achieved a harmony of purpose—love—had they been united. In rejecting Heathcliff, Catherine rejected, Fielding noted, a "completeness" of which she was only a part. Ultimately, however, she rejected that harmony which is a product of true love. Her rejection was an intellectual one; for her very being demanded Heathcliff, not Linton. Her intellect drew her to the tinsel glitter of Thrushcross Grange and its pallid life, for in its world she thought she would find herself and discover the other "dimension" that she intuitively sensed she lacked.

The point is significant because it plays so strong a role in Fielding's novels. All of his central figures are searching for love and for the existence it gives to the lover and the beloved. Their problems arise out of a confusion created by their intellects as those intellects mature: they pursue love intellectually rather than intuitively, and they are betrayed. Love has been distorted for them by too-analytical an approach. Mocking them and projecting their agonies are the structures Fielding creates which, through their balance, suggest the harmony of life. These structures suggest the unity, balance, and dimension for which his principal figures yearn; and his answer is that the peace and wholeness for which they grasp can be theirs if they could but grope for it intuitively.

There are, however, deeper implications in Fielding's analysis of *Wuthering Heights*. He senses in man's too heavy reliance upon his intellectual powers the essential problem confronting him in this age. "Man," Fielding writes, "is a refugee in a nightmare. [He] is lost inside himself, [he] wanders in a landscape in which all is inconstant and beyond understanding."[16] Man wanders bewildered because the god he has created—his own intellect—has betrayed him; it has not given him the path to and the knowledge of the rightness and the balance of life that he had known intuitively in previous, less intellectually oriented periods in his history. Fielding cites the age of Shakespeare and the Middle Ages as periods in which man was at ease with life, periods when no reconciliation between mankind and life was necessary because there was no division, periods when man had "belief . . . whole and unfragmented." Now man lacks vision because he has reoriented the universe and made himself, rather than Providence, its center.

As for what the "sense of the grandeur of Providence" can do for man, Fielding writes: "When Adolph Eichmann sat in his crystal box in Jerusalem to be tried, bewildered, for crimes of such enormity that they still remain meaningless to us, what we really needed was the vision which would have given us an exact knowledge of his responsibility and some inkling of our own. This can only be had through a sense of the grandeur of Providence, and the conviction that, in the end as Juliana of Norwich said: 'All will be well, and all manner of things will be well.' "[17]

This passage expresses the hope of modern man, and Fielding's personal function as an artist is to draw sympathetically and intuitively from his readers, by means of real and deeply felt experience, the truth that there exists a Providence and that ultimately "all will be well." His message is, therefore, an essentially spiritual one. But he hastens to indicate that his work is not a part of the growing coterie of writers—such as Graham Greene, Patrick White, Muriel Spark, and Günter Grass—who are attempting to revive a "spiritual tradition" in literature; for they react with "over solemnity" to man's predicament in this twentieth century. Moreover, they "seem to trust God so little that their characters have to bear the entire burden of holiness . . . and this reflects an almost universal absurdity . . . that of expecting more . . . than is fair or rational."[18]

Fielding disassociates himself from this group because he believes that the presence of evil and the depiction of it in human nature is necessary but "without the yardstick of failure you [have] no means of judging success."[19] Consequently, Fielding does not shirk the responsibility he feels to present evil in his novels. This evil, essentially sexual irresponsibility and hypocrisy, however, is presented clinically and coolly as his critics have noted. As might be anticipated, Fielding rejects not only the "spiritual" writers but also the "nowhere and nothing" ones whose works "have lost relevance by giving us no certainty to which we may safely cling" and who believe in "the concept that man is lost and can no longer distinguish between good and evil."[20] Instead, Fielding prefers to identify with those who have a sense of the totality of existence, who understand good and evil, heaven and hell, as integral parts of that totality, like Shakespeare in whose works "the lovers and the clowns, the murderers and kings, the mad and the sane, though not unaware of the devil knew how to deal with him. They played out their tomorrows against a backcloth which lent dignity and scale to the human situation. Though they knew what immortal longings were they were never denied the resurrection of intention and their passions were never petty."[21]

II *Fielding's Achievement*

For an adequate understanding of Fielding's achievement in terms of the contemporary literary scene, it is wise to turn to a concept of E. M. Forster in *A Passage to India.* Cecil Fielding, the principal of Government College at Chandrapore, listens to his Indian friend, Dr. Aziz, explain the method the Mogul emperors used to fill with water the tank by the mosque to Mrs. Moore and Miss Quested, visitors from England. The tank and the mosque have come to mean a great deal to Aziz, for there he had met Mrs. Moore on a moonlit night; and at that time the differences which had separated him from the English began to slip away because he had discovered their common identity and, in a sense, had come to love her. His explanation is merely an extension of that friendship, a deepening of that love. Although Aziz credits the Mogul emperors with the ability to reverse the pull of gravity—his explanation is that they were able to force the water to flow uphill to fill the tank —and although the principal knows that a depression of some depth lies in that part of Chandrapore and thereby could have exposed the lie, he does not expose his friend, though other Englishmen would have and thereby have proclaimed the superiority of their race who, manifestly, know the difference between fact and fancy.

Fielding understands this difference, but he does not care to expose his friend for another reason. His long sojourn in India—a land where "verbal truth" is less sought after than the "truth of mood"—has dulled his Anglo-Saxon craving for fact. He senses that Aziz is spinning about the ladies a veil of truth far more important and vital to their relationship than the false facts which bring it to life. Conjured before them are the ineffable beauty of the water as it lies before the mosque shimmering in the light of the moon; the equally glittering glory of the emperors, which grows with every reference Aziz makes to it; and ultimately, that gossamer veil, the veil of truth, which whispers to them that, despite their differences in sex, in race, in intellectual and emotional capacities, they are one even though a seemingly unbridgeable gulf seems to separate them.

This quality Gabriel Fielding the writer shares with Forster's character. The quality he attempts to project through his novels is intended to touch a world that appears bent on accenting the divisive aspects of human nature rather than the elements that unify it. The world focuses its attention on "truths," "facts," which conveniently and ironically ignore the higher truth that all men are one because of their common humanity. As a result of his purpose, Fielding belongs to that group of contemporary writers who probe the factual and verbal truths of man's existence in a world gone mad to draw from them an understanding of man's identity which he has discovered in humanity's need for and ability to love and be loved.

In this sense, Fielding ranks with his countrymen Evelyn Waugh, Graham Greene, Muriel Spark, Anthony Powell, and C. P. Snow, because he shares with them a similar concern for discovering this "truth of mood" through the dimensions of identity, which derives not so much from the fact of existence but rather from the atmosphere in which that existence takes shape. That atmosphere, these authors seem to indicate, is compounded from the place and the proportion of morality in the modern world: man's relations with and to his fellow man flow very directly from the pallid tastelessness of twentieth-century life.

Furthermore, like these writers, Fielding's stylistic roots are firmly imbedded in the English tradition of the novel. Though he is attracted by the patterns he senses in existence and reflects these patterns subtly, there is, nevertheless, a surface discursiveness that has become identified as the mark of the English novelist. This discursiveness, moreover, permits his characters to develop in very much the same manner as those of his forebear, Henry Fielding, or that of Lewis Eliot in C. P. Snow's massive *roman fleuve, Strangers and Brothers.*

Fielding is dedicated to the proposition that an individual is a composite of many facets: he is like a diamond, which has little or no life except as it meets and reflects an exterior light. In playing with and transforming, so to speak, that light, the diamond is revealed in all its glory; it is ever changing as it receives and reflects the rays of light yet, paradoxically, it is always the same. And so too is the light changed in a subtle manner as it meets the diamond and shatters into a rainbow of color. In a sense, the diamond and the light merge into a new being, a new existence. The one takes its new life from the other; the other, in giving of itself receives a new dimension; and the two are the more brilliant for their union. So too do Fielding's characters, like the diamond and the light, glow and glitter as they act, interact, and share a common character, which changes as the combination changes.

Fielding also projects a love of language, which he cherishes and displays much as a connoisseur inspects a piece of fancifully carved jade or an intricately crafted Japanese netsuke. Words for him have a life of their own quite apart from their meaning; this life confers existence upon their users. His characters are known, first, by their distinctive choice of language and, second, by the sharpness and terseness of their creator's verbal descriptions of them. Pithiness is, therefore, the essence of Fielding's style.

Yet, sweeping through the terseness of his pointed language is a mood that characterizes his work. This element is compounded by what he sees in the world about him—those facts which detract from the "truth of mood" he is attempting to establish—and by his emotional inheritance. He was reared in Yorkshire, and his memory of its moors and their sadness is as sharp and immediate as Emily Brontë's whose subject matter is not very different from Fielding's for both were nurtured on tales tinged with the bleakness of their surroundings. In a conversation, Fielding noted that his father's Yorkshire parish was far removed from the "prettiness" and "picturesqueness" of the Yorkshire seen by the tourist. The life was, instead, hard and unrelieved; and its tenor was matched in a sullen way by the climate. As a consequence, in Fielding's work as in Brontë's *Wuthering Heights,* joy is forever shadowed by the blackness of melancholia; happiness is always marred by the knowledge that death is inevitable. Again, like Emily Brontë, Fielding is also partially the product of Gothicism, a strain never truly dormant in the English temperament. He is fascinated, as is his contemporary Muriel Spark, by the strange and the bizarre. The scene in the cave in *In the Time of Greenbloom* and the scene in which Alfried is tortured in *The Birthday King* are examples of Gothicism at work, as is the half-real, half-grotesque world of *Eight Days.*

But Fielding's chief thrust is not controlled by Gothicism as is, perhaps, Muriel Spark's and, to a large extent, Graham Greene's. Fielding has a breadth of vision that cannot be contained within a single interest or within the scope of a single novel. In this sense, his work can be compared, as it has been by his critics, with that of Anthony Powell and C. P. Snow, both of whom have been occupied with the creation of *romans fleuves*—novels which flow on and on sharing a common plot and characters. Snow's series, *Strangers and*

Brothers and Powell's *The Music of Time* share a common focus: both attempt to construct a picture of the twentieth century, aiming not at verbal truth so much as at "truth of mood." Fielding's vision, like theirs, is dominated by a desire, "to take you through a stretch of our vexed, magnificent century: mind, place and event, doings and dreams, foibles and splendours. . . ."[22]

Fielding's purpose, therefore, is not involved with recording the facts of this century; for, though some of the great events of the age serve as backdrops for his novels, his desire is to establish the "truth of mood" that E. M. Forster projects so vividly in *A Passage to India*. This "truth of mood"—the spirit of the century which is Fielding's chief interest—is shaped and directed by many forces which, perhaps, have not been felt so keenly by novelists who are not English. Fielding, as an Englishman, belongs to a people who appear cold and unemotional to the foreigner; but, despite the effect they have on others, the English are not so much cold and unemotional as they are hesitant to reveal their emotions; for they are educated to practice the middle-class virtue of self-restraint. They understand the significance of events quickly, hence their ability to rule and to write penetratingly; but all too often they take too long to feel those events. Their immediate appreciation of fact is extraordinary; their immediate ability to project this appreciation emotionally is limited. As a result, they produced Victorianism and its child, Edwardianism, which Fielding senses have had too disproportionate a control over the affairs and ultimately the "mood of truth" of this century.

Therefore, Fielding's vision of his era develops in part out of an attempt to exorcise Victorianism and Edwardianism and the creatures and attitudes they have spawned: too great a concern for the surface facts and too little an appreciation of the realities of emotional existence. Like C. P. Snow's Lewis Eliot, Fielding's central figure—variously called John Blaydon, Alfried, Dr. Chance, or Pressage—is the epicenter of his vision of the world. The character's thoughts, emotional life, action, pain, and pleasure reflect and are molded by the facts of the twentieth century. Fielding's characters grow as the century grows; but they are shaped by his personal vision—one strained always through his personal experiences.

Like Powell and Snow, Fielding has not arrived at any absolute conclusions because he has much living and writing ahead of him. There are, nevertheless, indications of the proximate direction toward which his work will take him. This knowledge springs from the fact that his vision of life embraces a recognition of not only an earthly existence, but also —because his conversion to Catholicism has widened his vision—a supernatural destiny. This understanding, however, is never couched propagandistically as it sometimes is in the work of Greene and Waugh. Like these two novelists, Fielding understands man in terms of a moral and spiritual code which is broader, more inclusive, firmer, and more lasting than any established by an individual or a nation or a class of society.

Fielding also recognizes man's failure to live wholly by this spiritual code though he may subscribe to it intellectually. Despite man's failures, Fielding does not yield to the grim almost Jansenistic posture of Greene, nor to the corrosive satire of Waugh, even though he often calls upon these postures in shaping his work. Almost as often, his critics as a result have pointed out his debt to Greene and Waugh; but these critics have failed to indicate what Fielding has done to these influences, which he readily acknowledges. Greene and Waugh have failed to see life in the totality which Fielding brings to the novel and which, in turn, rescues his work from a sectarian label. Fielding's vision is one with Dante's who, despite the inconsistencies, stupidities, horrors, and tragedies he witnessed in life, knows instinctively and projects his knowledge subtly that God exists and that He is *"L'amor che move il sol e l'altre stelle"* —a love so great that it sets the sun and all the other stars in motion, a love so great that it enfolds and ennobles man and saves him from himself.

Notes and References

Chapter One

1. Unpublished lecture on *The Birthday King* delivered at Washington State University, November, 1968.
2. *Current Biography* (New York, 1966), pp. 127-29.
3. Roy Newquist, editor, *Counterpoints* (London, 1965), p. 196.
4. The Fieldings have five children: Michael (1946), Jonathan Milne (1948), Mario Simon George Gervaise (1956), whose godmother is Muriel Spark, Felicity Ann (1957), and Mary Gabriel Elizabeth (1960). Michael, a graduate of Oxford, is presently at the University of Michigan working for a doctorate in higher mathematics. Jonathan has recently received his bachelors degree from Washington State University. Both young men are aspiring writers.
5. Newquist, p. 205.
6. "The Longing for Spring Again," *The Catholic World,* CCIV (February, 1967), 297.
7. *Ibid.*
8. Newquist, p. 197.
9. Unpublished letter from Gabriel Fielding to Alfred Borrello, May 11, 1967.
10. "The Longing for Spring Again," p. 299.
11. Unpublished letter from Gabriel Fielding to Alfred Borrello, May 11, 1967.
12. *Ibid.*
13. "The Longing for Spring Again," p. 297.

Chapter Two

1. Advertisement for *Twenty-Eight Poems.*
2. Newquist, p. 203.
3. Unpublished letter from Gabriel Fielding to Paul Doyle, March 24, 1960, in Mr. Doyle's possession.

4. Evelyn Cavallo, "Gabriel Fielding: A Portrait," *The Critic*, XIX (December, 1960-January, 1961), 84-85.

5. Unpublished letter from Gabriel Fielding to Alfred Borrello, May 4, 1968.

6. p. 206.

7. Richard Hughes, *New York Times*, Book Review Section (May 14, 1963), p. 4.

Chapter Three

1. April, 1963, p. 90.

2. Unpublished lecture delivered at Washington State University, December 7, 1966.

3. Edwina Fielding, *Courage to Build Anew* (London, 1968), p. 22.

Chapter Four

1. December 24, 1958.

2. March 8, 1959.

3. *San Francisco Examiner*, March 18, 1959.

4. May 23, 1960, p. 210.

5. *Newsday*, March 21, 1960.

Chapter Five

1. February 17, 1959.

2. Unpublished letter from Gabriel Fielding to Alfred Borrello, September 25, 1968.

3. Anthony Burgess, *The Novel Now* (London, 1967), pp. 164-65.

4. Unpublished letter from Gabriel Fielding to Alfred Borrello, September 25, 1968.

5. *Ibid.*

6. *Ibid.*

7. Hughes, p. 4.

Chapter Six

1. "The Longing for Spring Again," p. 298.

2. Unpublished letter from Gabriel Fielding to Alfred Borrello, January 20, 1969.

3. *Library Journal* (June, 1966), p. 2872.

4. *America* (May 28, 1966), pp. 781-782.

5. September 2, 1966, p. 117.
6. June 24, 1966, p. 934.

Chapter Seven

1. "Sex, Symbolism and Modern Literature," *The Critic*, XXVI (August–September, 1967), 18.
2. *Ibid.*
3. *Ibid*, p. 21.
4. *Ibid*, p. 22.
5. Newquist, p. 200.
6. *Ibid.*
7. *Ibid.* p. 202.
8. *Ibid*, p. 203.
9. *Ibid*, p. 196.
10. *Ibid*, p. 201.
11. *Ibid*, p. 202.
12. *Ibid*, p. 199.
13. *Ibid.*
14. "Sex, Symbolism and Modern Literature," p. 22.
15. Newquist, p. 196.
16. "The Need for a Proper Evil," p. 6.
17. *Ibid*, p. 10.
18. *Ibid*, p. 8.
19. *Ibid.*
20. *Ibid*, pp. 6-7.
21. *Ibid*, p. 10.
22. Unpublished letter to William Morrow and Company, Publishers, August 17, 1959, in the collection of the publisher.

Selected Bibliography

PRIMARY SOURCES

1. Books. Both the British and American first editions are recorded. Also included are paperback and foreign editions.
The Birthday King. London: Hutchinson, 1962; New York: Morrow, 1963; New York: Signet, 1964; Milan, Italy: Bietti (under the title *il Re della Festa*), 1965.
Brotherly Love. London: Hutchinson, 1954; New York: Morrow, 1961.
Eight Days. London: Hutchinson, 1958; New York: Morrow, 1959.
Gentlemen in Their Season. London: Hutchinson, 1966; New York: Morrow, 1966.
In the Time of Greenbloom. London: Hutchinson, 1956; New York: Morrow, 1957; New York: Apollo Books, 1957.
Through Streets Broad and Narrow. London: Hutchinson, 1960; New York: Morrow, 1960.

2. Poetry.
The Frog Prince and Other Poems. Aldington, Kent, England: Hand and Flower Press, 1952.
Twenty-Eight Poems. Aldington, Kent, England: Hand and Flower Press, 1955.

3. Short Stories.
"After the Parrot," *The Critic*, XXVII (June–July, 1969), 38–40.
"L'Après-Midi, *Cornhill Magazine*, CLXVII (Srping, 1956), 353–87.
"Bravery," *Winter's Tales #2*, New York: St. Martin's Press, 1956, pp. 62–94.
"A Daughter of the Germans," *The Critic*, XXIII (August–September, 1964), 49–58.
"The Dear Demesne," *The Critic*, XXI (April–May, 1963), 21–24.

"Figs in Spring," *Winter's Tales #6*, New York: St. Martin's Press, 1960, pp. 1–21.

"The Young Bloods," *Vogue*, CXXX (October 15, 1957), 93ff.

4. Articles and Interviews.

"Angels and Artists," *The Critic*, XXI (December 1962–January 1963), 27–29. Discusses the choirs of angels and suggests that they have a fitting place in today's world but most particularly in psychiatry since their demon counterparts lurk in the id: superego, paranoia, mania, euphoria, etc.

"Evelyn Waugh and the Cross of Satire," *The Critic*, XXIII (February–March, 1965), 53–56. An analysis of the art of Evelyn Waugh with the conclusion that the "aridity" of *Gilbert Pinfold* was the price Waugh paid for his satire. "Anger is the cold core of Waugh's art."

"The Faint Noel," *The Critic*, XXIV (December 1965–January 1966), 38–41. A reminiscence of the Christmases of his youth and a condemnation of England as "an agnostic island of pragmatists."

"Graham Greene: The Religious Englishman," *The Critic*, XXIII (October-November 1964), 24–28. Greene's work "personifies the secret values of a decrepit, lost-Victorian generation."

"The Longing for Spring Again: an Interview," *Catholic World* CCIV (February 1967), 296–300. A discussion of Fielding's art centering on *Gentlemen in Their Season*. Fielding indicates that Waugh and Graham Greene influenced the direction his work has taken.

The Need for a Proper Evil, Chicago: Friends of Literature, 1967. Fielding calls for a balanced view of the world in which an understanding of good and evil is understood, as Shakespeare understood them, in terms of life's totality.

Newquist, Roy, editor, *Counterpoint*, London: Allen and Unwin, 1965, pp. 195–208. A discussion of Fielding's philosophy, his evolvement as a writer, his theories of literature and his Faith.

Fielding, Edwina, *Courage to Build Anew*, London: Burns and Oates, 1968. Preface by Gabriel Fielding. Fielding describes his first encounter with Aylesford, the pre-Reformation Carmelite Monastery destroyed by Henry VIII, and the Carmelites who rebuilt it.

"Sad Men Who Yet Rejoice: Gabriel Fielding on the Pubs in His Life," *The Listener*, LXX (August 29, 1963), 315. (Reprinted as "My Three Pubs," *Harper's Magazine*, CCXXVIII [January

1964], 24ff.) Identifies three of his favorite London pubs.
Discusses, fondly, their characters and their moods.

"Sex, Symbolism and Modern Literature," *The Critic*, XXVI
(August–September, 1967), 18–22. A discussion of contemporary literature in terms of the depth of concern given to
matters of sex and the application of decorative but superficial
symbolism.

"Splendid Old," *Harper's Magazine*, CCXXX (February 1965),
104–06. The death of a friend causes the author to meditate
on the aging processes. He discovers, in that meditation,
that he longs for a "wholeness" in his own old age.

"The Uses of Fear," *Harper's Magazine*, CCXIV (February 1962),
92–95. As a novelist and as a physician, Fielding analyzes
the reasons why one must learn to live with his fears and
offers suggestions on how one can make them work for him.

"Westward on the Bookbeat," *Nova* (September 1966), pp. 107–11.
A description of the promotion campaign for *Gentlemen in
Their Season* revealing American attitudes to books and their
authors.

"Who Shall Cure the Doctor," *The Listener*, LXXVI (November
24, 1966), 772–73. Discusses the plight of the medical profession in England.

Woolf, Cecil and John Baggerley, editors, *Authors Take Sides on
Vietnam*, New York: Simon and Schuster, 1967, p. 34.
Fielding deplores the war noting that unrestricted capitalism
is a luxury that evolving societies can no longer afford. Conversely, Communism with all its defects, however, is part of
the political and social evolution of mankind.

SECONDARY SOURCES

1. Books and Articles.

Bowers, Frank, "The Unity of Fielding's Greenbloom," *Renascence*, XVIII (September 1966), 147–55. Analysis of the structure of *In the Time of Greenbloom;* likens it to a symphony.

Burgess, Anthony, *The Novel Now*. London: Faber and Faber,
1967. Attempts to place Fielding within the context of the contemporary novel in English. Finds his *Birthday King* an
"extraordinary" work.

Cavallo, Evelyn, "Gabriel Fielding: A Portrait," *The Critic*,
XIX (December 1960–January 1961), 19–20ff. Describes Fielding's fiction as having an "all-enveloping aura of warmth"

when contrasted with Murial Spark's which has a "fastidious chastity of spirit."

GRANDE, BROTHER LUKE, "Gabriel Fielding: New Master of the Catholic Classic?" *World*, CXCVII (June 1963), 172–79. Suggests that Fielding may be the successor of Evelyn Waugh and Graham Greene in the field of the Catholic novel.

KUNKEL, FRANCIS L., "Clowns and Saviours: Two Contemporary Novels," *Renascence*, XVIII (Autumn 1965), 40–44. Discusses *The Birthday King* with Günter Grass's *The Cat and the Mouse* and discovers that Alfried Weidman is a "conventional Christ-clown figure."

2. Reviews.

(Only major reviews are noted in chronological order after the title of Fielding's work.)

The Birthday King

Times Literary Supplement (London), October 12, 1962, p. 797.

Derek Stanford, *The Critic* (April 1963), p. 70.

Richard Hughes, *New York Times*, Book Review Section, April 14, 1963, p.4.

Sylvia Stalling, *New York Herald Tribune*, Books, April 21, 1963, p.3.

Thomas Curley, *Commonweal* (May 3, 1963), p. 172.

Whitney Balliett, *New Yorker* (May 18, 1963), p. 174.

Newsweek (May 20, 1963), p. 105.

Martin Price, *Yale Review* (June, 1963), p. 608.

Brotherly Love

Daniel Wickenden, *New York Herald Tribune*, Books, August 27, 1961, p. 12.

Whitney Balliett, *New Yorker* (September 23, 1961), p. 174.

David Dempsey, *New York Times*, Book Review Section, October 1, 1961. p. 4.

Max Cosman, *Commonweal* (October 13, 1961), p. 78.

Eight Days

Times Literary Supplement (London), November 28, 1958, p. 685.

William Bittner, *Saturday Review of Literature* (February 28, 1959), p. 20.

Chad Walsh, *New York Herald Tribune*, Books, March 8, 1959, p. 6.

Jean Holzhauer, *Commonweal* (May 20, 1959), p. 654.

Gentlemen in Their Season

Paul Pickrel, *Harper's Magazine* (June, 1966), p. 98.

William Ready, *Library Journal* (June 1, 1966), p. 2872.

Times Literary Supplement (London), June 23, 1966, p. 549.

Robert Taubman, *New Statesman* (June 24, 1966), p. 934.

In the Time of Greenbloom

Sylvia Stallings, *New York Herald Tribune*, Books, June 9, 1957, p. 1.

Time (June 10, 1957), p. 104.

Isabelle Mallet, *New York Times*, Book Review Section, June 23, 1957, p. 21.

Alice Saxon, *Commonweal* (June 28, 1957), p. 331.

Through Streets Broad and Narrow

Max Cosman, *Commonweal* (June 3, 1960), p. 260.

Peter Green, *New York Times*, Book Review Section, June 12, 1960, p. 6.

Paul Scott, *New Statesman* (October 1, 1960), p. 492.

John Coleman, *Spectator* (October 7, 1960), p. 531.

Times Literary Supplement (London), November 11, 1960, p. 721.

Index

Index

164

ABOUT THE AUTHOR

In addition to this present volume, Alfred Borrello is the author and editor of five other books, including *A Concordance to the Poetry in English of Gerard Manley Hopkins, An E. M. Forster Dictionary, An E. M. Forster Glossary, H. G. Wells, Author in Agony*, and *E. M. Forster: An Annotated Bibliography of Secondary Materials*.

Dr. Borrello is Associate Editor of *The Evelyn Waugh Journal* and has contributed articles to *English Literature in Transition*. He is currently planning a critical study of E. M. Forster. Since 1969 Dr. Borrello has taught at Kingsborough Community College of the City University of New York as Professor of English.